postmodernism

Thi

Glenn Ward

0

TEACH YOURSELF BOOKS

Dedication

This book is dedicated to Louise Dennis, who helped me finish it, and Charlotte Barton, who got me going.

Every effort has been made to trace copyright for material in the book. The author and publishers would be happy to make arrangements with any holder of copyright whom it has not been possible to trace successfully by the time of going to press.

For UK orders: please contact Bookpoint Ltd, 39 Milton Park, Abingdon, Oxon OX14 4TD. Telephone: (44) 01235 400414, Fax: (44) 01235 400454. Lines are open from 9.00 – 6.00, Monday to Saturday, with a 24 hour message answering service. Email address: orders@bookpoint.co.uk

For U.S.A. & Canada orders: please contact NTC/Contemporary Publishing, 4255 West Touhy Avenue, Lincolnwood, Illinois 60646 – 1975 U.S.A. Telephone: (847) 679 5500, Fax: (847) 679 2494.

Long-renowned as the authoritative source for self-guided learning – with more than 30 million copies sold worldwide – the *Teach Yourself* series includes over 200 titles in the fields of languages, crafts, hobbies, sports, and other leisure activities.

British Library Cataloguing in Publication Data
A catalogue record for this title is available from The British Library

Library of Congress Catalog Card Number: 96–72383

First published in UK 1997 by Hodder Headline Plc, 338 Euston Road, London, NW1 3BH

First published in US 1997 by NTC/Contemporary Publishing,
4255 West Touhy Avenue, Lincolnwood (Chicago), Illinois 60646 – 1975 U.S.A.

The 'Teach Yourself' name and logo are registered trade marks of Hodder & Stoughton Ltd.

Copyright © 1997 Glenn Ward

Typeset by Transet Limited, Coventry, England.
Printed in Great Britain for Hodder & Stoughton Educational, a division of Hodder Headline Plc, 338 Euston Road, London NW1 3BH by Cox & Wyman Ltd, Reading, Berkshire.

Impression number   10 9 8   7 6   5 4
Year   2004 2003 2002 2001 2000 1999

CONTENTS

PREFACE

———— The aims of this book ————

Despite its title, you can't 'teach yourself postmodernism' in the same way as you can teach yourself economics, upholstery or the rules of chess. You don't have to master a specific set of skills in order to be able to 'do' it. Nor are there strict rules and requirements to memorise which will qualify you to be a fully fledged 'postmodernist'. Whatever postmodernism may be, it isn't exactly a discipline, activity, ability or pastime. That is not to say, of course, that there is nothing useful to learn about postmodernism. Far from it. I wrote this book with the conviction that it puts forward a number of ideas and debates which are both stimulating and worthwhile. I hope this will become apparent to you too, as you read the book.

As we will see, one of the difficulties, but also perhaps one of the strengths, of postmodernism is its sense of fluidity and open-endedness. It resists being conveniently summarised in easy 'soundbites' and refuses to lend itself fully to any single cut and dried definition. So this book does not aspire to 'solve' postmodernism. It pretends to be neither definitive nor totally comprehensive. Rather than being an encyclopaedia of postmodernism, it is a guide to the territory which sets out to provide you with useful points of entry and orientation. To that extent, and in order to avoid confusion and congestion in its very limited space, it has to take a selective view. This inevitably means that some aspects are covered in more depth than others, and that there are some things which I have decided to leave out completely.

But being necessarily partial is not the same as being narrow. One of the problems with introductory texts in this area is that they often give an account of the 'postmodern condition' from a single angle, or from within the limits of just one academic field. They may, for example, take *either* a literary or a sociological approach to the postmodern. The danger here is that the perspective on postmodernism given by one subject area does not necessarily correspond to or illuminate what it means for another. One outcome of addressing a more specialised audience in this way is that it can seem rigid and insular to the general reader. To avoid that problem I have tried to take a more cross-disciplinary approach. This book therefore introduces as wide a range of ideas, thinkers and views as is possible without losing focus.

Using this book

Chapters have been organised around broad themes and concerns rather than around individual ideologies, schools of thought or art-forms. This should allow you to tailor the subject matter to your own interests and requirements. The book probably makes most sense when read from cover to cover, but individual chapters are designed to be coherent by themselves and can be read in an order of your own choosing. It is hoped that, especially if you make use of the index, you will find echoes from thinker to thinker, follow your own threads and make new connections.

Some of the theorists discussed here can be a struggle to read. I do not claim that what follows will miraculously transform their writings into works of incredible clarity. They will remain difficult. But this book will give you a grip on many of the key ideas wrapped up in their notions of the postmodern. In that respect you can treat it as a self-sufficient statement in its own right. But my desire is that, having used this book, you will want to go beyond it: I hope that it will have provided a framework of ideas through which to carry out your own investigations.

1
POSTMODERNISM

The fact that you have picked up this book suggests that you have heard of postmodernism, and perhaps that you would like to know what it means. Maybe you already have an idea of the kinds of thing that it refers to, and would like to find out more about it. Or perhaps you find it utterly confusing, and want to be furnished with a definition. Either way, it is hoped that this book will fulfil these needs.

In this chapter we will look in a very general way at the significance of the word postmodernism. We will begin by looking at why the meanings of postmodernism sometimes seems so hard to grab hold of, and will go on to examine some of the ideas behind the word.

—— Postmodernism is everywhere ——

Over the last two decades the term *postmodernism* has been in widespread use, but the story of its spread through culture is fairly complex. Apart from a number of isolated early sightings of the term (some of which we will discuss later in this chapter), it started life mainly as an academic category concerned with certain developments in the arts, but soon became a descriptive term for all sorts of proposed shifts and changes in contemporary society and culture. To take just one example, it was argued that the world had lost faith in technological progress. Because faith in technological progress was seen as belonging to a specific 'modernist' historical period, the term 'postmodernist' was thought an apt description of our new period of disillusionment.

However, by the mid 1980s, postmodernism had blossomed into what can sometimes seem like a catch-all term for just about anything.

By the middle of that decade, postmodernism in many areas (like architecture, politics or literature) was frequently discussed in late night television 'culture' slots, radio arts programmes, and middle-brow Sunday newspaper supplements. These discussions often consisted of either agonising over what sense could possibly be made of a word like postmodernism, or dismissing it outright as a trendy buzz-word rapidly reaching its sell-by date.

Today, the deluge of books on postmodernism has slowed to a steady drizzle, and heated debate has cooled into sober reassessment. In some quarters (the art world for instance) the word, if not the issues to which it refers, seems to be in the process of being wilfully forgotten. Meanwhile, aspects of postmodern theory have been fully integrated into humanities courses right across the western world.

The persistence of postmodernism

So postmodernism persists, to the extent that we might almost say (again with a little exaggeration) that it has become part of everyday speech. Let's take some random examples. An article in a British journal devoted to horror films, *Necronomicon*, recently described 'slasher movies' as a postmodern phenomenon. References to it can now crop up in a comic way in lager commercials in a spoof of 'arty types', advertisers being confident that their target audience is aware of the *word* postmodernism, if not exactly of its *meaning*. And in a TV soap it would not now be out of place for the 'boffin' or 'bookworm' character, probably in an attempt to impress someone, to drop postmodernism into the conversation. The fact that this would be played for laughs is very much to the point. For what would count in both places is post-modernism's *status*, rather than what it might be *about*. In order to make fun of the types of people who talk about postmodernism – in order to use the word as a sign of 'braininess' or pretentiousness – script writers must assume that viewers have heard of it. Without this kind of awareness, the word can serve no purpose, comic or other-wise. Another example of this occurred on British television a while ago when the host of a family game show was inclined to throw the word into his patter. These examples begin to suggest that postmod-ernism may be in the process of settling into everyday language. And this in turn suggests that it might be worth our while to look into exactly what lies behind it. *Teach Yourself Postmodernism* is a guide to doing so.

Multiplying meanings

It is possible to look at the field of psychoanalysis, identify its founding figure as Sigmund Freud, and go on to describe the main conceptual tools behind the psychoanalytic method. With postmodernism it is not quite so easy to do this. Postmodernism is not, strictly speaking, a school of thought. It is not a unified intellectual movement with a definite goal or perspective, and it does not have a single dominant theoretician or spokesperson.

This is because ideas about postmodernism have been adopted by virtually every discipline, from philosophy to cultural studies, from geography to art history. Each area has produced books and periodicals with their own particular angles on the topic, each has defined postmodernism in their own terms. In short, postmodernism has proliferated. Taken on board in so many different fields, where it can refer to so many different things, its meanings have multiplied, and the sheer volume of texts it has generated in this multiplication have tended to obscure, rather than clarify, what on earth it is all about. The problem is that what postmodernism might mean in one discipline is not necessarily compatible with what it might mean in another.

So postmodernism now leads a complicated life. So complicated, in fact, that there are really several postmodernisms in existence, or at least many variations on it. On the one hand it is beginning to circulate, however ironically, in popular culture. On the other hand, it remains a controversial subject in specialist academic books and journals. Some areas have become bored with it and are looking for alternatives. Others are only just getting used to having it around. For some, it is now a firmly established shorthand for a range of social and cultural transformations. Still others remain sceptical about its usefulness.

Even in the day to day speech of what are sometimes called the 'chattering classes' postmodernism has more than one application. It can be used, for example, as a vague term for any contemporary artefact that seems in some way ironic. Or it can be used, even more vaguely, as a general name for our particular moment in history. Add to this the fact that its meaning has been argued over in the very areas (such as literary criticism) in which it was born, and postmodernism seems ever more resistant to definition. Perhaps the only certain thing is that postmodernism is hard to get to the bottom of.

A flexible term

All of this might make it sound as though postmodernism can be anything you want it to be, and perhaps there is a little truth in this. In ways which this book will demonstrate, postmodernism can be:

- An actual *state of affairs* in society
- The *set of ideas* which try to define or explain this state of affairs
- An artistic *style*, or an approach to the making of things
- A *word* used in many different contexts to cover many different aspects of all the above.

These are just four of the ways you can think about what postmodernism is. There are probably others. Of course, it is not so easy to separate these approaches in practice. For instance, if there is such a thing as a postmodern artistic *style*, a theorist of postmodernism might look at how that style relates to, or arises from, a defined postmodern *condition* in society.

Although taking something from all of them, the second approach in the above list is closest to the one adopted by this book. Rather than attempt to offer one all-embracing definition, postmodernism is most fruitfully viewed as a variety of perspectives on our contemporary situation. This means seeing postmodernism not so much as a thing, more as a set of concepts and debates. We might even go so far as to say that postmodernism can best be defined as that very set of concepts and debates about postmodernism itself.

New times

Despite its great flexibility, postmodernism is not meaningless, and ways into it are not so hard to find. Of course, it still has the connotations of obscurity and elitism that always seem to stick to words with a so-called intellectual origin. But although theories about it are often discussed in very abstract terms, postmodernism can equally be concerned with far more concrete matters.

There are a number of identifiable themes which run consistently through the different versions of postmodernism, and the chapters of this book have on the whole been organised around them. Put as broadly as possible, these themes are to do with what it means to live in our present times, and with how best to go about describing them.

- They propose that society, culture and lifestyle are today significantly different from what they were a hundred, fifty or even thirty years ago.

- They are concerned with *concrete* subjects like the developments in mass media, the consumer society and information technology.

- They suggest that these kinds of development have an impact on our understanding of more *abstract* matters, like meaning, identity and even reality.

- They claim that old styles of analysis are no longer useful, and that new approaches and new vocabularies need to be created in order to understand the present.

So postmodernism can be about finding ways of describing the world as much as about that world itself. To this extent, postmodernism can be seen as unfinished. It can be seen as an ongoing project to find new ways of looking at new times.

Pre-history

Perhaps the biggest problem with postmodernism is the word itself. The prefix *post-* means *after*, and *modern* can be taken to mean *current* or *up-to-date*. How then is it possible to be *after* the *modern*? How can we get a handle on such a paradoxical notion? One thing we can do is look at some of the word's history.

Although postmodernism's boom time has been in the last decade or two, it has actually been around for quite a while. The term did have a number of isolated early incarnations, and these make up a kind of 'pre-history' of postmodernism. Before we go on to look at some of them, it is worth remembering that we should not see such 'pre-historic' examples as definitive. To do so can sometimes lead you up blind alleys, because what postmodernism meant *then* does not always sit comfortably with what it means *now*. Having said that, the six examples given below are worth looking at because they do overlap in some interesting ways with today's varieties of postmodernism. As we will see, they do anticipate to a certain extent the terms and debates of the more recent, more fully developed postmodernisms. Attempts by historians to discover the first ever use of the term have so far been inconclusive, but early appearances include:

The 1870s

An English artist called John Watkins Chapman used it to describe painting which he saw as more advanced than that of French Impressionist painters like Claude Monet or Auguste Renoir. The work of the Impressionists had been seen as the very latest up to the minute expression of modern times – in other words as the most *modern* of modern art. In Chapman's usage, postmodernism referred to new (post-Impressionist) art which went further than Impressionism's attempts to capture in paint the fleeting appearances of nature.

1917

The German writer Rudolph Pannwitz spoke of nihilistic, amoral new 'postmodern men' who had broken away from old established values of modern European civilisation.

1947

In his summary of British historian Arnold Toynbee's six volumes of *A Study of History* (1947) D C Somervell suggested that Toynbee's focus on history could be called 'post-Modern'. Toynbee then took it up, and in subsequent volumes of his work he put forward the notion of a 'post-Modern age'. This age was the period following on from the Dark to Middle Ages (1075–1475) and the Modern Age (1475–1875). The 'Modern' was regarded by Toynbee as a time of social stability and progress. But since about 1875 western civilisation, with the growth of industrialised cities, had been troubled by social turmoil, anxiety and revolution.

1957

American cultural historian Bernard Rosenberg named as postmodern the new circumstances of life in society at that time. He argued that important social and cultural changes were taking place. These changes included the rise of technological domination and the development of a mass culture of universal 'sameness'.

The work of Rosenberg, Toynbee and others provides a good example of how early uses of the term postmodernism do not always tally with how it is used today. In their work, changes in the values and conditions of society were effectively brought about by the expansion of industry. Their use of the term postmodern to describe this expansion was both specialised and potentially confusing. Specialised, because it was meant to draw attention to the contemporary world's difference from certain political, economic and philosophical aspects of the 'Modern' age. Potentially confusing, because the period of transition from one era to another (roughly the late nineteenth to early twentieth centuries) is more usually known as the period of *modernity*. We will come to describe the features of modernity in more detail in a moment.

1964

Leslie Fiedler described a 'post-' culture which rejected the elitist values of highbrow modern art and literature.

1968

American art critic Leo Steinberg noticed in contemporary visual art (for example, Pop Art) a change in interest from the representation of nature to the 'flat' representation of man-made images. He called this tendency postmodern because whereas older kinds of modern art (from Impressionism onwards) had been concerned with capturing visual or emotional truth, Pop Art was interested in artificiality.

There are two important areas of overlap between these various 'prehistoric' postmodernisms and the meanings of postmodernism today. The first concerns the notion that we have entered a phase in history with its own unique characteristics. The second concerns an important distinction (but also an equally important mingling) between theories of postmodernism in society, and theories of postmodernism in the arts. Both of these aspects are surveyed in the rest of this chapter. Though brief, this survey will provide some orientation for our later explorations.

—— Modernity and enlightenment ——

Some of our postmodern forerunners spoke about society entering a new phase. They claimed that we were in a historical period with novel features that distinguished it from any other time in history. In particular, it was to be distinguished from the preceding Modern Age. The exact character of this age, as well as the precise dates of its beginning and end, has been described in different ways by historians, but it is often associated with faith in:

- Progress

- Optimism

- Rationality

- The search for *absolute knowledge* in science, technology, society, and politics.

- The idea that gaining knowledge of the *true self* was the only foundation for all other knowledge.

In debates about postmodernism, these kinds of value are often called *Enlightenment Ideals*. In other words, they are associated with the *Age of Reason* (or Enlightenment) which originated in seventeenth and eighteenth century Europe, and which quickly influenced all western thought. As the above list suggests, early Enlightenment ideals involved rational enquiry as the guiding principle for all knowledge, and the belief that only progress in intellectual method could bring about a world of order, security, social understanding and happiness.

This so-called *enlightment project* or *project of modernity* is not without its own internal disagreements, of course; it involves as many doubts and disputes as any other historical phase. To this degree it may be something of an over-statement to speak of the Modern Age (in Toynbee's sense of the term) as having, or being, a single project. Nevertheless, the general philosophy of the period is often defined in terms of its belief that progress in society could be brought about through the gradual perfection (through increasing self knowledge and rigorous intellectual method) of humanity. Thinkers associated with this tradition include Kant, Hegel and Voltaire. The up side to it was an investment in universal human rights that ultimately led to the French Revolution and the United States' Declaration of Human Rights. The down side to it is that, in believing that their values should be universally applied, Enlightenment thinkers tended arrogantly to see Europe as the most enlightened and advanced part of the world. Europe was seen as more civilised than the rest of the globe, and this led to the dangerous feeling that other countries and races could be colonised, exploited or bettered. As we saw in the case of Arnold Toynbee, some early accounts of a *post*-modernism describe a decline in these values or a radical break from them.

This proposed decline or break also forms an important part of today's debates about postmodernism. It is often argued that today's society has lost sight of these ideals. In direct contrast to the above features of the Modern Age, postmodern society is often negatively associated with:

- Exhaustion
- Pessimism
- Irrationality
- Disillusionment with the idea of absolute knowledge.

To confuse matters even further, the Italian author and theorist of culture Umberto Eco has seen, as a result of these supposedly widespread features of the present historical moment, a return in our times to attitudes of the middle ages.

On the other hand, many postmodern thinkers, rather than regretting the fall of the enlightenment, have actively sought to challenge its assumptions or have celebrated its supposed decline. As you will see, this has been the case with most of the thinkers dealt with in this book, and hopefully their reasons for doing so will become clear as we go along.

—— Modernity and modernisation ——

Another name for the Modern Age is *modernity*. Modernity is connected to the idea of modernisation. Modernisation suggests updating something, or bringing something into line with what are seen as present day fashions and needs. If we talk, for example, of having our kitchen modernised, we mean that we are having it fitted with the latest equipment and decorated in a more 'now' style (of course, having a 'now' style these days might involve having a very 'tomorrow' (futuristic) or 'yesterday' (Olde Worlde) style. Likewise, modernisation of the workplace (whether shopfloor, classroom, hospital or office) usually consists of keeping it up to date with current technological innovations and of putting into practice the latest ideas about achieving efficiency and maximum productivity. Similar processes of modernisation can be seen in most walks of life, from medicine to town-planning to education to telecommunications. It is, of course, an endless process. No sooner is an innovation put into service than it is modified or replaced by a newer, better model. Hence styles in clothes and kitchens will always be going out of fashion, washing powders will forever be 'new and improved', and employers will always find ever-better ways of 'streamlining' their workforce. Such a dynamic of constant and rapid change has been accelerating especially since the turn of the nineteenth and twentieth centuries.

In or after modernity?

These and other factors have all been seen as part and parcel of a unique stage in social history – a period featuring many important differences between traditional and contemporary society. To this extent, the society we live in now can be interpreted as the result, or as the intensification, of the key features of modernity outlined above. It seems clear, for instance, that new ways of communicating are still being developed (the fax machine, the Internet, and the mobile phone are three fairly recent examples), that cities are continuing to grow upwards and outwards, and that the updating process is (at least in areas like fashion) as rapid as ever.

For these sorts of reason, some versions of postmodernism (both pro- and anti-) have seen it not as a break, but as an outcome or extension of modernity. Postmodernism in this case is to do with what modernisation has so far led to – postmodernism as the latest point in the progress of modernisation. For example, we see in the sixth chapter of this book how recent developments in cybernetic technology can be linked to theories of postmodernism. Yet these developments can be seen as the most recent product of the process of endless invention triggered off by the Industrial Revolution rather than as part of a unique contemporary historical epoch that at some recent point simply snapped off from the past.

To take another example, television has sometimes been seen almost as a symbol for postmodernism itself. Television today, with its satellite broadcasts, channel surfing, live reports from war zones and so on, can indeed seem like a unique innovation. But it can just as easily be seen as a product of the rise of mass media that began in the final quarter of the nineteenth century. It was at that time, for instance, that Marconi invented telegraphy, and the Lumière brothers developed cinematography out of a whole array of photographic experiments and discoveries. Thus, for all its apparent newness and technological sophistication, television today can be seen as another product of modernity. Some of the aspects of television that have recently attracted the attention of postmodern theorists will be dealt with later in this book, especially in the fourth chapter.

The question of whether postmodernism is a split from an older era, part of an endless cycle of change, or just another aspect of the Modern Age (perhaps with a genuine postmodern period yet to come) has been a focus of considerable debate. Opinions on it depend largely on how the timetables of history are drawn up. They depend on where people draw their lines between and around so-called periods of history. As any theorist of postmodernism would argue, such periods exist more as man-made ways of carving up the past and the present than as real stretches of time with actual, momentous beginnings and endings.

Just as there is no straightforward way of drawing a line between the Middle and the Modern Ages, so there can be no clean, objective, distinction between the modern and the postmodern. We can point to no single date and claim that it marks either a chasm or a point of transition between the two periods.

A distinction

If you look back at our six early uses of the word postmodernism, you will see that it could be divided into two main categories. On the one hand, there was the concern with postmodernism as a *social and economic* event, brought about mainly by the spread of mass industry. On the other hand, there was postmodernism as what we might loosely call a *cultural* matter, a matter of changes in the arts.

In some ways this distinction between the social and the cultural is quite artificial. The two can be said to inform each other to such a degree that, in reality, they cannot be separated. Would you, for example, put television into the cultural or the social category? Again, why should the arts be considered as apart from the social? Despite this, it is a useful distinction to bear in mind when you start looking into postmodernism. For instance, recent novels that have been called postmodernist (novels by, say, John Fowles, Kurt Vonnegut or E. L. Doctorow) may be named as such because they reflect or express postmodern social conditions or because they have parallels with some postmodern factor found in other art forms. But they may also be called postmodernist because they can be said to come in an important way after literary modernism. Without having to define literary modernism for now (and it is quite a contentious matter), the point to note is that it is not *necessarily* the same as modernity in society at large.

Now, as you will have noticed from the above, a distinction can therefore be made between: postmodern*ism* and postmodern*ity*.

Technically speaking, the first refers to cultural and artistic developments (i.e. in music, literature, art, film, architecture, and so on), while the second has to do with social conditions and the 'mood' that these conditions give rise to.

Sometimes this distinction has been adhered to in postmodern theory, and sometimes it has not. Nowadays, however, postmodernism tends increasingly to be doing service for both sides. For the sake of consistency, I will tend to follow this practice of using postmodern*ism* to describe the two.

Conclusion

So far, we have looked at postmodernism in largely negative terms. We have looked at some of the confusions which continue to surround it despite, or because of, its popularity. We have indicated some of the general trajectory of postmodern theory, and we have made some suggestions about what postmodernism is not. What we have avoided so far is one clear, single definition of what it *is*.

When people ask what postmodernism is, they often seem to be asking for the word to be used as a name for a single, observable thing. That thing may be an object, a human condition, or whatever. Either way, it is something that is assumed simply to exist. The postmodernism label, it is assumed, can then be unquestionably stuck on to it. The thing can be defined, and we can all go home happy, secure in our knowledge of what postmodernism is. However, many theorists of postmodernism would argue that things do not really happen that way. They would argue that unquestionably postmodern things are not just going about the world waiting to have their postmodern credentials objectively identified by you or me. To name something (whether a theory, artwork, or aspect of society) as postmodern is not simply to unearth an objectively existing truth about it. Nothing contains a retrievable 'essence of postmodernism' which you can drag into the light and examine for clues to postmodernism's ultimate nature or genetic code. Rather, if you call something postmodern, you are placing it into a certain category, or framing it in a certain way. You are bringing an idea *to* it, rather than discovering a quality *in* it. In doing so you are ultimately linking it to a set of ideas about the world and our relationship to the world.

So postmodernism is most usefully thought of as an elastic critical category with a range of applications and potential understandings. It is a kind of 'portable' term which enables us to enter a great many ideas about the specific characteristics of the world today. Some of these ideas have only been hinted at so far, and the rest of this book is devoted to unravelling them.

Further reading

You can find more about the Enlightenment, its ideas, and the postmodern challenges to them in:

Postmodernism: A Reader, edited by Thomas Docherty (1993)
The Enlightenment and its Shadows, edited by Peter Hulme and Ludmilla Jordanova (1990).

2
ARTS OF IMPURITY
– PART 1

Introduction

In this and the chapter which follows we will look at aspects of the art, architecture and literature produced recently which have been given the 'postmodern' label. Our main aim will be to be look at what we might loosely call *cultural relations* or *the politics of culture*. That is to say, we will look at how postmodernism is involved in questioning the relationships between different aspects of cultural life. The kinds of question postmodernism asks in this respect are:

- What is the relationship between what we call art and what we call everyday life?

- What relationship does art have (and what relationship *should* it have) to the mass media?

- What is the relationship between 'high culture' and 'low culture'?

- Is it still (and has it ever been) valid to define cultural life in terms of this hierarchy of high and low, or is the 'map' of culture more complicated than that?

- Is it possible to make value judgements about the tastes of others? How is it possible? And why would you want to?

This chapter will look in fairly general terms at how these sorts of issue have affected both the theory and the practice of architecture and literature. Chapter 3 will concern itself in rather more detail with the world of contemporary art. These two approaches will:

- Define some of what *modernism* has come to mean in the arts

- Demonstrate how the idea of *postmodernism* can take hold within a specific area, and in the process become central to debates about the issues outlined above

- Tell us what postmodern *style* is sometimes said to be, and why it looks the way it does

- Lead into some of the broader ideas addressed later in the book.

The critic Andreas Huyssen has suggested that modernism in the arts defines itself as necessarily outside of, and superior to, the rest of culture and society. Postmodernism, on the other hand, crosses the great divide that modernist art and criticism once tried to place between themselves and mass culture. For various reasons, that supposed split between high and low has become less and less relevant to many artists and critics since at least the 1960s. For Huyssen, postmodernism represents a rejection of modernism's 'relentless hostility to mass culture', and moves towards a new situation in which 'the pedestal of high art and high culture no longer occupies the privileged space it used to'. This means that while the role of the arts is, for Huyssen, to maintain a critical stance towards contemporary society, they no longer do so from an imagined position of superiority.

Postmodernist arts have their feet more firmly on the ground and recognise that they share the same world with all other aspects of cultural life.

Let's see how this works in practice.

The Demolition of Modernist Architecture

If you have recently visited an in-town shopping centre built at some point in the last fifteen or so years, there is a good chance that it had at least some of the following characteristics:

- A mixture of architectural styles from past times (perhaps you can find echoes of Victorian greenhouse, art deco cinema, georgian and so on)

- A mixture of styles from different places: American-style diner, Italian-style pizzeria, London pub, Breton crêperie)

- Numerous ornamental, decorative or pictorial features (murals, reliefs, pediments, clock towers, columns that don't hold anything up)

- Lots of play between different surfaces, materials and colours (marble effects, plexi-glass, mirrors, unconcealed girders, smooth plastics, wood, plastic wood, chrome)

- A high degree of 'fake' (tap any interior column and it is likely to make a hollow sound; examine any flagstone floor and you are unlikely to find it made of real stone)

- A high degree of 'referencing' (as well as referring to the styles of different times and places, the exterior of the building might echo the shapes and materials of the surrounding area).

As you will have guessed, all of these features can be, and often have been, defined as postmodernist. That is to say, they represent a departure from the rules and conventions of modernist architecture. Modernist buildings, generally speaking, are easy to identify. Think of any large grey office block, factory, or housing development constructed between the 1950s and the mid 1970s, and you will probably have in mind a classic example of high modernism at its most depressing. It probably features the following:

- Repetition of a simple shape (squares, rectangles, boxes)

- Uniformity of design (mostly the same all over)

- Complete lack of frills (no ornamentation)

- Harsh, industrial looking materials (especially reinforced concrete)

- A flat roof (totally impractical in wet countries)

- Dominance over the surrounding environment (very big, towering over older buildings, neighbourhoods were probably flattened to make room for it)

- An imminent demolition order.

The contrast between this and your town's latest shopping arcade is probably quite stark.

Many such modernist edifices are now being pulled down. Yet not so long ago they were considered the future of urban planning, the pinnacle of architectural progress. Hard as it seems to believe in the light of all that we now know about shoddy construction, 'concrete cancer', high crime rates, vandalism, and the discomfort of living in an anonymous box in the sky, the perpetrators of this style of architecture saw themselves as part of a genuinely *Utopian* impulse – a belief that modernism could play a central part in the improvement of human life. But one of the first major demolitions of a modernist development was as long ago as 1972, when the Pruitt-Igoe housing project (completed in 1955) was declared uninhabitable and was subsequently dynamited by the city of St. Louis, Missouri. This event has famously been identified by one postmodern architect, Charles Jencks, as the day modernism died. We will return to Jencks in a moment.

Modernist architecture

Modernism in architecture is generally identified with a small number of European and American architects working in the early part of the twentieth century: Mies van der Rohe, Walter Gropius, Henri Le Corbusier, and Frank Lloyd Wright. Their ideas rapidly spread on a global scale. Many of the techniques, as well as the appearance, of their buildings were adopted by architects all over the world, becoming the familiar *International Style* which we caricatured above. Although there are differences between their ideas, the main thrust was a belief in:

1: Novelty

It is necessary to be 'up to date'. Architects should express the spirit of the modern, industrial age, and not be tied to the past. The new world has its own, dynamic qualities and architecture should both speak of and contribute to this dynamism, unfettered by tradition. It should make maximum use of new building materials and methods.

Engineers are new modern artists. The art of architecture is now a matter of maths, science and function. Buildings should be streamlined, *rational* machines. Being rational means that they should be based on rigorously scientific (as opposed to subjective) reasoning. Housing should be based on the same design principles as factories and automobiles. Modern cities should be designed to accommodate speed.

2: Progress

Humankind can only escape from misery by shedding the past and embracing the age of the machine and mass production. In uniting industry, science and art, rationalising the organisation of urban social spaces and sweeping away the congestion of the old city streets, modern architecture can create Utopia. This will be achieved on an international scale, with no thought for backward-looking, stifling regional traditions. New communities can be quickly built on the basis of cheaper materials and standardised units. Modernity is technological progress; industrial manufacturers and machine designers are engaged in a search for universal harmony and perfection. Architecture should participate in this evolution towards a bright, hygienic, efficient society.

3: Heroism

Modernist architects see themselves as the god-like creators of a brave new world. They have privileged access to the keys to the advancement of civilisation, and so they draw the blueprints of the future.

4: Purity

This Utopian vision is to be achieved through the strictest of means. Buildings are to be reduced to their purest forms. Their beauty lies in their function, simplicity, rationality, newness and unity. Beauty is not something tacked on to them in the form of decoration. Ornament is to be rejected as superficial, dishonest and wasteful. Modern building must be 'true to itself'. Frivolous trappings serve only to detract from a building's integrity.

As you can see, this all links directly back to the points we made about the modern Enlightenment project in the previous chapter. This can be summarised as the belief that the progress of the whole world could be spearheaded by the superior, more rational knowledge possessed by the Western intellect. The rest of the world could be literally civilised by the values that the International Style represented.

Modernism's Utopian project is in sharp contrast to our picture of monotonous, grey 1960s tower blocks being served demolition orders, and some see this as testament to the failure of modernism. In post-modernism, the modernist faith in rationality, purity, and visual honesty is replaced by playfulness, mixing and blatant artificiality. Instead of idealised notions of expressing the spirit of the age or of forging the way into the future, we now have overt (perhaps ironic, perhaps nostalgic: how can you tell the difference?) references to the past.

Elitism?

Some criticisms of postmodern architecture

Some critics have seen postmodernism as representing a failure of nerve on the part of architects. They have regarded it as a decline in standards, a conservative appeal to the lowest common denominator, and a collapse of the artistic imagination. From this point of view, although postmodernist buildings do embrace the latest construction techniques and materials, their designers have lost their modernist bottle and run out of revolutionary spirit. Swapping their moral and aesthetic responsibilities for cheap populism, they no longer see their activity as vital to the creation of a better tomorrow. Postmodernist architecture is therefore regressive rather than progressive, reactionary rather than radical: a sell-out of all that architecture should stand for.

According to this view the way postmodernism mixes references is hollow. It is all empty show. It has no respect for the sources of its quotes, no real awareness of history. Like a television viewer switching channels through remote control, you are shown nothing but visual sound-bites. It is yet another product of a culture with a three-second attention span – a culture which takes nothing seriously. This reflects a general tendency in our culture to be simultaneously obsessed with images of the past and forgetful of real history. (Similar criticisms are often made about theme parks, heritage parks, shops which sell imitation bygone goods, and television costume dramas.)

Another criticism is that the postmodernist principle of mixing playful references in one building is mostly only applied to places of business, leisure and/or shopping, while housing design generally remains as unimaginative as ever; postmodern architecture is therefore just a way of trying to get people to spend more time at the shops.

Defence of postmodernist architecture

Others would see this as a welcome turn away from delusions of grandeur. The picture of modernist architects knowing what is best for the masses and for the rest of the world and seeing themselves as the guardians of true aesthetic values is a disturbingly arrogant, elitist one. Consider the following examples:

- The Pruitt-Igoe development was demolished because its low-income residents so disliked the prize-winning modernist accommodation they were forced to endure that they repeatedly vandalised it.

- In Britain a number of similar housing developments have recently been proposed as listed buildings of historical and artistic interest. This will mean that no city council will have the authority to dynamite them. Needless to say, many residents interviewed on TV news were appalled to find that their homes were deemed aesthetically significant by middle-class tastemakers who did not have to live in them.

In both of these examples it can be argued that modernist architecture is based on a view of the inherent superiority of high culture over the tastes of ordinary people.

In addition, it can be argued that modernist architecture was never wrong in principle. Well-made modernist buildings can and do offer people considerable material comforts. It is just regrettable that so many bad ones were constructed.

Plural Coding

The architect and theorist Charles Jencks has praised postmodernist architecture for its ability to go beyond this kind of modernist elitism.

Modernist ideas aimed to strip architecture of ambiguity and connotation. They stated that a building should carry no associations outside of its own magnificent declaration of modernity. Jencks calls this aspect of the modernist ideal *univalence*. What he means by this is that buildings were supposed to have a single meaning. For example, the International Style preferred buildings to be structured around the repetition of a simple geometrical formula.

One problem with this was that modernist buildings often failed to give pleasure to their users (the exception being luxury houses commissioned from modernist architects by wealthy patrons for private use). Against this, Jencks proposes that postmodernism is *multivalent* (has many different meanings) or *plural coded*. That is, it is deliberately open to many different interpretations. Instead of imposing a single meaning, formula or presence on anyone, postmodernist buildings are more free-style and allow for the pleasures of finding associations and making connections. They have little respect for whatever might be regarded as architecturally pure or correct, preferring instead to reach out into the wider cultural arena of which they are a part. They therefore try to effect a greater sense of communication.

To take one of the most well-known examples: in the A.T. & T. building in New York, designed by Philip Johnson, a classical broken pediment perches on top of what appears to be a typical case of high international modernism (a rather imposing oblong skyscraper). The building as a whole can be said to refer (at least for those who get the references) to a modernist skyscraper, a particular Italian Renaissance chapel, Chippendale furniture, and even the radiator of a Rolls Royce. Modernist critics will be unlikely to take much of an interest in A.T. &T.'s resemblance to a grandfather clock. Being a modernist, they will be keen to study its harmonious orchestration of forms and materials, rather than what these might allude to. The rest of us can take pleasure in resemblance to other things, or in the effect of mixing ancient and modern in a single building.

You can of course find equally good examples in any town today: ironically enough, plurally coded postmodernism has itself become a new sort of international style.

The function of postmodern architecture

A.T. & T. building, New York © Joe Kerr, the Architectural Association

So postmodern buildings are collages of different visual styles, languages, or codes. They allude at once to local traditions, popular culture, international modernism, and high-technology, yet refuse to let any one of these elements become dominant. Jencks argues that by mixing and mis-matching in this way, plurally coded architecture opens itself up to a wider audience. It is a form of 'dissonant beauty' which, full of vitality, ambiguity and irony, defines different functions according to the needs, tastes and moods of different social groups. It speaks in many accents in order to engage as many 'readers' as possible, all of whom will be able to read the language of the building in their own terms, relating it to their own knowledge and experience.

In this way postmodern architecture is a democratic 'juxtaposition of tastes and world-views' which responds to the fact that we live in what Jencks sees as a pluralistic, cosmopolitan 'culture of choice' rather than one of enforced sameness. This theme of *cultural diversity* occurs frequently within postmodern theory and practice. It will reappear several times in the rest of this book (see, for example, the discussion of Jean-Francois Lyotard in Chapter 8).

Jencks argues against the criticism, sometimes levelled against postmodernism, that it is necessarily a conservative or merely nostalgic tendency. He claims that postmodernism, rather than simply regurgitating tradition, can be seen as a 'radical eclecticism' which actively engages in a dialogue between past and present, showing (contrary to the modernist myth of absolute novelty) that each affects our understanding of the other. He also argues that, by colliding different codes, postmodernism highlights the different ways in which buildings can be read into by diverse 'taste cultures'. They show, against modernist ideology, that meanings are never absolute or universal. According to this argument, the idea that there are timeless or universal aesthetic truths which we should all learn to appreciate is the product of a privileged social group (the modernist 'taste culture') with a specific area of knowledge and a particular agenda. Ideas about purity and progress and beauty are far from neutral: they are cover-ups for the social, historical, and political positions of power from which architects draw up their designs.

Conservative and radical postmodernisms

As the above account implies, postmodern architecture is sometimes divided into *radical* and *conservative* categories. Jencks distinguishes between:

Straight revivalism

Buildings in this category are those which are simply old fashioned. Any building which is new but looks old fits this description. Jencks sees this sort of architecture as a problem because instead of challenging tradition it simply repeats it. It is unquestioningly stuck in the past.

Radical eclectism

The kind of architecture which Jencks puts into this category mixes up styles and references in an ironic way. By placing different styles together it effectively puts buildings in quotation marks, expressing a more critical attitude both to tradition and to architecture itself.

Another critic, Fredric Jameson, has found a similar two-part categorisation within the entire field of postmodern culture. He distinguishes between:

Pastiche

Echoing Jencks' view, Jameson likens uncritical, nostalgic revivalism in architecture to 'speech in a dead language'. It is a form of quotation, with no sense of irony or satire. It pieces old styles together, but only because it can think of nothing better to do. Jameson thinks that pastiche is taking over as postmodern culture's dominant trait.

Parody

This is a mimicry of old styles again but, unlike mere pastiche, it mocks rather than merely plunders from tradition, and has a critical edge.

A query

Is that new shopping mall or multiplex cinema on the outskirts of your home town critical or uncritical? Was that Quentin Tarantino movie an example of parody or pastiche? Try to think of your own examples which seem to fit Jameson's and Jencks' distinctions. Then ask yourself just how easy it is to distinguish between these terms in practice. How do you tell a style that is critically quoted in a building from one that is merely nostalgic? Do the distinctions really work? Are they as clear cut as Jencks and Jameson think they are?

Further Reading

Two useful books by Jencks are:

What is Post-Modernism? 1987
The Language of Post-Modern Architecture, 1991

———— Looking to Las Vegas ————

Despite all the above, Charles Jencks shows some sympathy towards the modernist theme of steel, concrete and glass cubes. His democratic 'something for all the family' approach to buildings means that modernist style still has a place. Modernists are still valid for Jencks; he simply does not want a single architectural lexicon to take over.

Another important theorist of postmodernist architecture is Robert Venturi. He tends to go further than Jencks in seeking to erase elitism from building design and urban planning (indeed, he argues that urban sites should be planned as little as possible).

Like Jencks, Venturi has no interest in creating a proper, pure style devoid of humour or playfulness. Instead, he champions the ways in which constructions are adapted to local circumstances through everyday processes of customisation and personalisation. He urges architects to reject the idea that ornamentation is artistically wrong, and to respect instead the variety of ways in which people gain meanings from their environment. He believes that building design should aim for communication and meaning rather than for streamlined perfection. Influenced by Pop Art (see next chapter), he finds vitality and significance not in *essential forms*, but in what modernists would see as the superfluous and trivial.

Venturi and his colleagues look at commonplace, regional building traditions for inspiration. He also looks at the streets of Las Vegas as the greatest embodiment of what he describes as a truly democratic, non-puritanical architecture. In Las Vegas Venturi discovers a dynamic interplay between diverse signs and textures. In place of one aesthetically correct blueprint imposed by a single heroic modernist expert, cities like Las Vegas revel in clutter, complexity and 'vital mess'.

Venturi favours urban sprawls, 'decorated sheds', clichés, and the proliferation of images which he drives by on the American open road, to
the dry modernist monument. Rather than being static and domineer-
ing, this urban sprawl presents itself as a story – or mixture of stories
– continually being re-told. Though disliked by orthodox architects
and design review boards, urban sprawl can be read as a continually
mutating process of creative response to current needs and to readily
available materials.

Venturi praises 'the urban manifestations of ugly and ordinary architecture'. He sees billboards, flashing signs, facades, blatant commercialism, anachronistic combinations and hot-dog-shaped fast food counters
as generators of meaning and experience rather than as lapses in good
taste. Venturi would not, for example, be scornful of a British suburban
home-owner who attached a decorative 'olde- worlde' cartwheel to the
front of their house. Rather than diagnose a serious case of aesthetic
misconduct, as some modernist critics would, he would see a creative
bit of collage, a sign of individuality, a deliberate resistance to the
elitist puritanism of society's would-be tastemakers, and a desire to
connect with the past. In short, he would find there a 'symbolism of the
ordinary'.

Two key books are:

Learning from Las Vegas by Robert Venturi, Denise Scott Brown, and
Steven Izenour, 1972 (revised 1977)
Complexity and Contradiction in Architecture by Robert Venturi, 1966
(revised 1972)

Literature: close that gap

Modernism within the institutions of the arts often rests on ideas
about its relationship with low, mass or popular culture (for the sake
of convenience, I will use these three terms interchangeably). Many
versions of modernism present high and low culture as two very distinct spheres: there might be degrees of influence from one to the
other, but they are essentially worlds apart.

In his book *Postmodernism and Popular Culture* (1994) the

Australian cultural historian John Docker uses the British literary critic F.R. Leavis (1895–1978) as a prime example of a particular kind of modernist attitude. In books like *For Continuity* (1933), Leavis sketches a view of a discriminating, minority culture which is the standard-bearer of all that is artistically and morally proper. Leavis proposes that a small handful of English, American, and European writers – including Shakespeare, Dante, Ezra Pound, T.S. Eliot, Virginia Woolf and James Joyce – represent the 'finest consciousness of the age' and he sees it as the job of critics like himself to promote their superior works. The connection here with the arrogant self-perception of the modernist architects is hopefully quite clear: both see themselves as having superior insight into what is best for people, both think that they know what kinds of art people ought to have.

Although the writers championed by Leavis are quite diverse, he argues that what they all have in common is a rejection of over-sentimental subject-matter and over-pretty writing styles. Again there are parallels here with modernist architecture's hatred of the frivolously decorative. Leavis sees his literary hall of fame as characterised by intellectual rigour, subtlety, and wit. When he discusses writers of the modern period, Leavis makes much of the fact that they are in touch with the language of the contemporary world. However, the point of this concern with everyday life is not to celebrate or participate in it, as seems to be the case with Robert Venturi, but to subject it to criticism. In Leavis' view the role of modern literature is to oppose modern society and the cliché-ridden (and often 'Americanised') products of its mass media. Elite, minority culture must constantly be on its guard against the spread of Hollywood, advertising, 'pot-boilers' and other manifestations of facile popular culture. Film is a particularly disturbing influence because it mesmerises its audience with cheap and easy pleasures.

On this view, the mass art of the industrial age is characterised by commercialism and standardisation, and these pose a serious threat to art's single-minded pursuit of timeless values. The modern world distracts people with so many forms of mindless entertainment that they are tempted away from art's traditional, more authentic standards.

By contrast, it is often argued that postmodernism tests the boundaries between what gets called high and what gets called low culture. It asks us whether such distinctions are still valid today (if they ever were), and it asks us to question the grounds on which such distinctions are made. It recognises that contemporary society offers a vast range of different forms of entertainment, but it is less concerned with defending the 'ivory tower' against them.

Within the field of literary studies, one of the several different movements often put forward as a milestone on the road to a postmodernist attitude is Leslie Fiedler's 1969 essay *Cross that border – Close that Gap*. Fiedler celebrates contemporary writing – such as that of Philip Roth and Kurt Vonnegut – for its ability to open the doors of the ivory tower. Where critics like Leavis had presented 'high' literature as a monolithic treasure-house surrounded by a sea of trivia, Fiedler promotes a postmodernist literature that is flexible, *pluralist* and *hospitable to the popular*. The crucial issue for Fiedler is that most assessments of literary merit are secretly rooted in social class structures. He hopes that with postmodernist writing and criticism it will become possible to judge quality in a way which does not depend on the class-based hierarchy of high vs. low.

A brief criticism

One of the more confusing aspects of the distinction between modernist and postmodernist literature is that you can find overt references to low culture in both of them. For example James Joyce's 1922 novel *Ulysses* is often seen as a classic modernist text, yet it combines self-consciously high literary styles with steamy romantic fiction and journalistic prose. Meanwhile, novelists like Umberto Eco and Kurt Vonnegut are seen as postmodernist because they *refer* to popular forms like science fiction and the detective novel.

The difference is sometimes said to be a question of motives. When modernists refer to popular culture, it is in order to mock it or improve upon it. They may even take the occasional holiday in popular fiction – they might, for example, try to liven up the 'academy' by taking prose styles from advertising or best sellers – but they still see high culture as the best place to be.

When postmodernists do the same they are said to be welcoming the plurality of contemporary cultural life with open arms. However, being seen to welcome or quote popular culture is not quite the same as being seen as popular culture. For instance, Vonnegut is said to refer to popular science fiction. Could he not just as easily be seen as a popular science fiction writer?

In some commentaries on postmodernism, testing the high/low border is still presented as a top-down issue – a specific problem for art more than for our thinking about the wider culture. The question often remains 'what is our art going to do about popular culture?' The hierarchy therefore stays pretty much in place.

Further reading

Some useful extracts on postmodernism in literature, including one from Fiedler, can be found in: *Postmodernism; a Reader*, edited by Patricia Waugh (1992)

A useful and thorough exploration of literary modernism is *Modernism*, edited by Malcom Bradbury and James McFarlane (1976)

The cultural mix

Consider:

Advertising has become a new art form. Many television and cinema commercials are now more imaginative, vibrant and exciting than much high art.

Many commercials also make reference to the world of art, but a lot of art equally makes reference to the world of advertising. What's the difference between them?

What *is* popular culture anyway? How many people a year need to visit your national museum of modern art, and buy postcards of the art from the museum shop, before it can be called popular?

Many commercials use classical music. Many film soundtracks (particularly horror films) are indistinguishable from experimental modernist music. Record shops are full of classical music, world music, pop music, rock, easy listening and so on. Many of us are comfortable in several different musical worlds. We are not usually restricted to just one taste. We often make our own compilation tapes which happily mix any number of 'levels' of music. Modernist critics might try to tell us what we ought and ought not watch, read and listen to, but most of us are much more eclectic (and much less puritanical) than that; we consume a very diverse range of goods offering many different experiences.

On radio, television, video and home computer the whole of world culture seems to be at your fingertips. The media, it has been argued, are placeless imaginary spaces which refuse to make clear distinctions between things. Adverts for ice cream and sun block interrupt an art history programme. Moving into different realities can be done at the push of a button. Everywhere you look, different, perhaps contradictory, messages, images and ideas jostle for attention. In this new media domain, anything can go with anything, like a game without rules. Or, at least, you can make up your own rules: culture can no longer be administered, there is no legislation about what can and cannot be consumed. Modernists would bemoan this as a slackening of aesthetic criteria. Postmodernists would agree, but would say 'good thing too'. They would ask, exactly whose criteria were they in the first place? And why should anybody have taken notice of them?

Flattening the hierarchy

❛ Once upon a time there were the mass media, and they were wicked, of course, and there was a guilty party. Then there were the virtuous voices that accused the criminals. And art (ah, what luck!) offered alternatives, for those who were not the prisoners of the mass media. Well, it's all over. We have to start again from the beginning, asking one another what's going on ❜

(Umberto Eco *Travels in Hyperreality*, p.150)

I have on my desk as I write this a newspaper article expressing doubt about the fact that, as it argues, everything from anoraks to sofas to refrigerators to cars are now all equally treated as cultural phenomena by cultural theorists. This, it suggests, reveals a complete draining away of definition or judgement, an inability within postmodern conditions to tell the significant from the insignificant or the good from the bad. But even if this is true, *does it matter*?

Looking at the sorts of example we listed above, some recent writing on postmodernism has argued that the high/low model provided by Leavis and many others is no longer an appropriate way of looking at things. As the quote from Umberto Eco suggests, you can no longer accurately represent culture as two distinct levels. The map of cultural life has been re-drawn. In fact, postmodern culture *is* this new map. There is, for example, no self-evident reason why Bach should be seen as better than Bacharach. This is not necessarily to say that they are the same, just that they are equal. Everything swims in the same social sea of signs, images and meanings.

So critics and theorists need to stop thinking of culture as a building with two storeys. Culture is in a sense flat rather than hierarchical: it is a *horizontal field* in which different areas of interest mix, converse, cross over and sometimes fight with each other. It is not a vertical edifice in which influences and/or disagreements travel up and down between the top (art and literature) and bottom (mass or popular culture) floors.

Further reading

For some interesting attempts by postmodernist critics to describe 'what's going on', as Eco says, see:

Uncommon Cultures: Popular Culture and Postmodernism, by Jim Collins (1991)
Postmodernism and Popular Culture by John Docker (1994)

3

ARTS OF IMPURITY – PART 2

Introduction

In this chapter we will see how some of the themes of postmodernist architecture and literature (see previous chapter) have been developed in visual art. The aim is two-fold. Firstly, it will give us further understanding of what modernism has meant within some areas. Secondly, it will allow us to explore in some detail how the idea of postmodernism can become the focal point of debates within a particular field of activity. Because it is impossible to cover all the issues and approaches adequately within a single chapter, this will be a partial view of what postmodernism has meant in the art context. However, it is worth noting that many of the issues discussed in other chapters have also had a considerable impact on the art world over recent decades.

A note of caution

Any attempt to define postmodernism simply in terms of a single style or period is unlikely to work. There is no single point at which postmodernism springs into being, and it is hard to find a contemporary approach to art that does not share ideas with much earlier twentieth-century work. Another difficulty is that modernism itself tends to resist simple summary. In the first place, it was manifested differently in different countries and movements. Add to that the fact that modernism is still in the process of being redefined in retrospect by *post*modernism, and it is clear that the proposed differences between the two are far from cut and dried.

With these warnings in mind we can begin by summarising the 'official' account of the modernist legacy. I will then offer a potted history of postmodernism in art. The intention is that these will provide a context for the more detailed examination which follows them.

Make it new!

Most descriptions of modernism in art tend to date it from the mid to late nineteenth century, with the development of impressionist and post-impressionist painting in France (Monet, Degas, Gauguin). This is often described as the beginning of a great experimental period in art, a period in which art pursued new goals and broke free from all traditions of representation. In this simplified view of events, the impressionists triggered off a break from the past in which art learned to turn away from realistic styles of representation and move towards more abstract forms of expression.

In this revolution art progressed by means of 'heroic' experimentation – the shock tactics of the 'tradition of the new' – towards a position of highly self-conscious *art for art's sake*. The idea behind this was that art should become valid for its own sake, without having to have any relation to the visual world. Via the innovations of cubism (starting with the work of Pablo Picasso and Georges Braque, around 1907) and abstract expressionism (most often associated with American painting of the 1940s and 1950s by Jackson Pollock, Mark Rothko and others), along with many other movements, modernism is sometimes said to culminate in certain highly reductive (minimalist) art forms of the 1960s and early 1970s.

Many of the key terms in the definition of modernism in visual art recall those in architecture. They are the ideas of:

- experimentation
- innovation
- individualism
- progress
- purity
- originality

Modernism in art can be broadly defined as heavy investment in these ideas.

Playing among the ruins: a
— brief history of postmodernism —
in the art world

In the following short section I offer an overview, painted in very broad strokes, of what postmodernism has meant for recent art. This will provide a backdrop to the more in-depth discussion which follows it.

The term postmodernism first gained widespread use in the art world around the beginning of the 1980s. Although its accuracy as a description of the art receiving attention at that time was sometimes fiercely debated, it was generally agreed the term did at least signal that important changes were taking place in art.

Up until that point international art journals and big collections of contemporary art had been full of rather austere stuff. Although there had always been maverick presences around, the art that tended to be taken seriously by the 'official' (New York centred) art establishment was generally quite cerebral and dry. Various forms of minimalism in the 1960s and 1970s, for example, reduced sculpture and painting to the simplest forms and processes (bricks, cubes, slabs, grids, squares, flat fields of colour). Much conceptual art of the same period was similarly unseductive: monochrome photographs juxtaposed with bland text, holes made in gallery walls and artists performing endlessly repetitive 'actions' were the order of the day.

Things changed around 1980. Suddenly it became fashionable to do huge, splashy paintings *of* things. Representations of the human figure made a comeback, and in the context of an economic boom-time for the art world, a number of prominent new (usually male and pretty macho) artists made fortunes painting them. Although welcomed as a return to common sense by more traditional art critics, this supposed return to painting was greeted with dismay by other artists and critics who liked to think of (modernist) art as the cutting edge of all that is progressive and experimental in culture.

This early version of postmodernism was associated with a pluralist, 'anything goes' attitude and an obsession with the past. Old styles and techniques were re-hashed and artists quoted from the work of other artists. Abstract art was still pursued but this had a more ironic, tongue-in-cheek edge than was usually expected of abstraction. Art became more playful and (occasionally) entertaining.

This was all taken as a negation of the progress of art, with minimalist and conceptual art seen as a dead end. Art had reached the end of its progress. There was nothing new left to do. What act could possibly follow the recent spectacle of rows of bricks, piles of dirt and even empty art galleries being exhibited as art? For some there was a feeling that art had gone as far as it could go, leaving an endgame situation in which artists could choose only to re-tread art's earlier steps or to play with its left-overs. Others, as we will see, complained that art had been swallowed up by commercialism.

It was thought that instead of ceaselessly experimenting and offering uncompromising attacks on conventional ways of thinking about art and society, the new painting was a betrayal of all that modernism had stood for.

More cautious assessments suggested that ideas about progress, radicality and originality had been myths in the first place and were no longer sustainable in a complex, media-saturated society. Postmodernist painting could be seen as simply making the most out of the collapse of these myths. In a world orientated towards the media and mass communication, art had been made irrelevant – as an artist, you might as well just sit back and enjoy the show. On the other hand, the new painting could be seen as a lively challenge to dominant modernist ideas. It tested the assumptions of influential modernist critics, and it raised important questions about what it was that art was now supposed to do, and about how it was meant to do it.

More complex ideas about postmodernism quickly infiltrated the art world. Next to painting, photography and media based work regained the limelight in the mid 1980s by seeming to provide a more obviously political postmodernism. A number of artists working in this field were hailed for making a specifically feminist intervention in postmodernism. Other artists began to gain notoriety for producing three-dimensional pieces based largely on showing shop-bought goods. The question for postmodernism now was not, as it had been at the beginning of the 1980s, whether the progress of art had shrivelled up, but how artists should respond to mass culture. From this perspective, mass media and commodities were seen as the instruments of a corrupt capitalist system. If art was to have any purpose in the contemporary world, it had to set itself up in opposition to this system. How could they subvert (or even compete with) the power of the media? How could they oppose the world of commodities without becoming luxury goods themselves?

In order to answer these questions, it became necessary to re-forge the links between contemporary art, the conceptual art of the 1970s, the pop art of the 1960s and beyond. It also became necessary to examine the work of a number of predominantly European postmodern theorists. The work of the French thinker Jean Baudrillard, in particular, was often used in the service of the more media-conscious brands of postmodern art, and became something of a cult among art students in the 1980s. We will have a lot to say about Baudrillard's influential theories in the next chapter. By now, the idea that postmodernist art was just a nostalgic/humourous/cynical art of quotation seemed too simplistic.

In today's art world, the 'anything goes' attitude is no longer controversial, 'continental' theory is less fashionable, and the word 'postmodernism' rarely raises eyebrows. Nevertheless, many changes and issues heralded by the concept of the postmodern remain current.

Further reading

Valuable snapshots of the views and controversies of the early days of artistic postmodernism can be found in:

Beyond Modernism; Essays on Art from the '70s and '80s by Kim Levin (1988)
Art Talk: the Early Eighties edited by Jeanne Siegel (1988)

—— **Modernism and autonomy** ——

There is a number of widespread beliefs about art. One is that artists dedicate their lives to their art without any ulterior – especially commercial – motive. Another is that artists have unique insight into things. Finally, we often assume that art is somehow timeless. All of these beliefs suggest that art exists in a special realm outside of ordinary life.

Modernism similarly believes that art is essentially independent and self-governing. Although this idea of the autonomy of art has been expressed in many different ways, one of the most common is to propose that works of art are intrinsically different from all other sorts of objects. They are governed, if at all, by rules and interests not found elsewhere, and they provoke special kinds of response in their audience. Art does not have to justify itself economically, politically, morally, or in terms of its use. It is free from social convention. It is just art. One of the most influential statements of this attitude – and the one against which postmodern art and theory most often pits itself – is the work of the American art critic Clement Greenberg. Greenberg is known for a number of essays and reviews published in art journals between the late 1930s and the mid 1960s. Let's look at two of his most well known pieces, published in the left-wing arts journal, *The Partisan Review* in 1939 and 1940.

Towards a Newer Laocoon

According to Greenberg, every historical age has a 'dominant art form', and between the seventeenth and mid nineteenth centuries the dominant art form was literature. This means that literature became the prototype which all other art forms tried to imitate. For example, nineteenth century salon paintings tried to tell sentimental, melodramatic tales: in doing so, they were aspiring to the condition of literature.

This is an artistic crime in Greenberg's view. The aspiration towards literary effects in painting and other art forms is a lamentable 'confusion of the arts'. In this confusion, there ceases to be any reliable standard by which artists and critics can make judgements about quality. The aesthetic worth of a painting is a question that can only be framed in relation to the specific properties, conventions, and history of painting itself. To look at a painting's ability to tell a story or to imitate a three-dimensional object is to fail to look at it on its own terms. A painting is only a painting. It is not a book or a sculpture. This argument rests on the belief that the various art forms possess – or else should achieve – characteristics of their own which separate them from all other art forms. Greenberg insists that modern art progresses through the struggle of artists to boil their art down to its barest essentials and thus to achieve genuine quality. He calls this progressive refinement a process of rigorous self criticism.

Painting's process of self-criticism involves a number of innovations:

- abandoning shaded modelling and perspective
- emphasising brush strokes
- using harsh colours rather than subtle tonal changes
- stressing line (line is abstract because it doesn't occur in nature)
- using geometrical forms
- using 'all over' compositions
- simplifying forms.

In these ways, paintings stopped trying to fool people. Instead of pretending to be stories or windows on to another world, they called attention to the fact that they were just flat surfaces made of paint on canvas. Flatness was particularly interesting to Greenberg because being flat was the one thing which pictorial art did not share with any other art form.

Thanks to this new emphasis on materials – the *integrity of the support*, the *resistance of the medium* – painting triumphed over all the other arts. It most successfully defined its own unique essence. In doing so, it no longer had to justify itself. Like objects of nature, paintings were now their own justification.

Avant-Garde and Kitsch

Drawing in part from the British art critic Clive Bell, who wrote in 1914 that 'to appreciate a work of art we need bring with us nothing from life', Greenberg implied that in order to enter the space of art you must unburden yourself of social, political, practical and moral baggage. All of these things only hinder the perception of art as art. He notes that art is always surrounded by money, and that modernism was related to the expansion (in the middle of the nineteenth century) of an affluent middle class market for art. But for Greenberg economic and social factors like the existence of a system of patrons, galleries and collectors within a privileged class do not detract from the purity of the modernist enterprise – in fact, they simply create favourable conditions in which an autonomous art can flourish.

'True' culture is under constant threat from *kitsch*. There are two meanings of kitsch in Greenberg's essay. On the one hand, it is a sentimental sort of pseudo-art which rips off the products of 'quality' high culture. Perhaps we might think of certain performers of easy-listening music as fitting this description. Or in painting, we might think of certain artists who present 'painting for pleasure and profit' programmes on day-time TV. Greenberg would include bad high culture in this definition as well. The melodramatic paintings produced by many artists during the Victorian era would be singled out for particular contempt.

On the other hand, Greenberg also speaks with a mixture of disgust and amusement of 'that thing to which the Germans give the wonderful name of kitsch: popular, commercial art and literature with their chromeotypes, magazine covers, illustrations, ads, slick and pulp fiction, comics, Tin Pan Alley music, tap dancing, Hollywood movies, etc. etc.'. The only thing that these otherwise diverse art forms have in common is that they are all manifestations of mass or popular culture, and it seems that is reason enough for Greenberg to reject them. The only thing he leaves standing is something called 'art and literature of a high order' – namely that which achieves the supposedly self-validating status he had outlined in *Towards a Newer Laocoon*. 'High order' culture and kitsch are two separate worlds which cannot be reconciled. Any attempt to blur or cross the boundaries between them can only result in artistic catastrophe.

Presumably, if we do not recognise high order art when we see it then we, and not Greenberg's sweeping judgements, are at fault. In this respect his posture echoes that of the modernist architects and literary critics we encountered in the previous chapter. They all have incredible confidence in their own standing as arbiters of taste. They all seem to believe that they – unlike the rest of the 'common herd' – have their finger on the pulse of what is right and good in the field of culture. A postmodernist approach would see this stance as arrogant and deluded.

Summary

Art progresses, through the struggle of individual artists with their materials, towards a condition of self sufficiency and freedom. Art which lags behind or does not take part in this progress is of no interest.

The drive towards autonomy and purity in painting and other art forms is a kind of self-defence by authentic art against debased low culture. Visual art should not tell stories (or have 'content' in the usual sense) because that is literature's job and because kitsch art does it. Modernist painting draws attention to itself as medium or artifice. Kitsch doesn't. To achieve genuine quality the arts should each know their place.

Greenberg's modernism is *formalist*. What this means is that it is concerned less with whatever a work might be said to represent, and more with abstract matters like composition, material processes and visual stimulation. It rejects all interpretations not based mainly on the pure optical experience of art works.

Some postmodernist criticisms

In the last couple of decades there have been many criticisms levelled at Greenberg and at the general assumptions about art which his ideas represent:

- His art history is too selective. It picks and chooses only those few artists whose work seems to add to the neat story of progress he wishes to promote.

- This narrative serves nationalistic interests, in that it allows Greenberg to assert the status of American abstract painting and sculpture as a 'world beater'. For him art is like a race, with everyone running towards the same finishing post.

- He bases his argument on a simplistic picture of culture as a war between two worlds: avant-garde vs. kitsch. Culture is far more complex and multi-layered than this two-tier model can allow for.

- He is too prescriptive. He rejects out of hand any alternative ways of understanding works of art. All other academic approaches are seen as beside the point, and the pleasure people might get from finding associations in an abstract painting, for example, is marginalized as irrelevant and primitive. Enjoying art therefore becomes a matter of possessing certain skills. This serves only to mystify art, and to preserve its unreasonably high social status.

In fact, Greenberg's argument undermines its own case: in order to enjoy the *autonomous, purely optical experience* of an abstract painting, you need to have read plenty of modernist theory first.

Further reading

Many books are available which take issue with Greenberg's brand of modernism. Among them are:

Pollock and After: The Critical Debate edited by Francis Frascina (1985)
The End of Art Theory: Criticism and Postmodernity by Victor Burgin (1986)
Art and Discontent by Thomas McEvilley (1991)

—— Andy Warhol, postmodernist ——

The re-evaluation of Greenberg, and of the whole aspect of modernist theory he represents, has been a central project of postmodernism in art. But these criticisms are present in art practice as well as in art theory (some commentaries suggest that in postmodern art the conventional line between theory and practice has disappeared). Many artists could have served just as well, but I have chosen to look briefly at the American pop artist Andy Warhol (1930–87). This is mainly because his work has achieved a very high international profile outside of the confines of the art world, and not because he in any sense *invented* postmodern art.

Most people are familiar with at least some of Warhol's work. His various screen prints of Marilyn Monroe, produced during the 1960s, are very well known, often being reproduced on posters, greetings cards, calendars and so on. His Campbell's soup cans and cola bottles are nearly as famous. The trademarks of Warhol's art are fairly straightforward (and 'straightforwardness' is perhaps itself a Warhol trademark):

- mechanical reproduction of an image by means of photographic silk-screening on to canvas
- use of ready-made imagery from advertising, magazines, etc.
- repetition of a single image many times on a single canvas

Marilyn Diptych, Andy Warhol © ARS, NY and DACS, London 1997

- casually applied unnatural colours

- despite photographic sources, a lack of illusionism (perspective, realistic shading, etc.)

- non-correction of mistakes: many of the prints are mis-registered, too faint, too dark or simply crooked.

We should also mention Warhol's skill in becoming a media icon, his ability to generate hype, and the way that his art has crossed over into more mainstream culture (in addition to postcard and tee-shirt reproductions of his best known images, many adverts imitate Warhol's visual style). As well as being a hugely successful fine artist, Warhol worked at various points as an illustrator, film maker and producer, magazine editor, and band manager; contrary to the modernist myth of dedicated struggle with a single medium, Warhol was quite at ease in a range of different roles.

Seeing double: Warhol's postmodern 'hybridity'

In Greenberg's terms, Warhol's work represents a *confusion of the arts*. It uses popular images and sources within an art context, and semi-industrial techniques in a context that traditionally values original one-offs. It exists between screen-print and painting, original and copy, handmade and reproduced, abstraction and representation, and, most importantly, high and low culture.

Certain aspects of Warhol's work can be made to fit comfortably into Greenberg's prescriptions for modernist painting. It uses unrealistic colour schemes, flat areas of colour and all-over compositions. It is deliberately artificial-looking and makes no attempt to conceal the process of its making.

By producing work that was apparently hospitable to an abstract modernist interpretation, Warhol was able all the more quickly to succeed in the contemporary art market. By seeming to attain certain Greenbergian standards, he soon entered the pantheon of important, highly collectable modern artists.

But unlike the kind of modernism discussed above, Warhol's work was deliberately impure in that it combined these abstract procedures with mass culture images. It provided ordinary, non-modernist people with images they (as well as Warhol) could identify with. As with Charles Jencks' postmodern multivalent architecture (see Chapter 2),

Warhol's art respects the validity of different taste cultures. It is open to the plurality of experiences and understandings that different groups can invest in images. This openness is in marked contrast to the modernist's elitist sense of expertise. To quote Howard Fox:

❻ Far from seeking a single and complete experience, the post-modern object strives toward an encyclopedic condition, allowing a myriad of access points, and infinitude of interpretive responses ❺
(quoted in *Postmodernist Culture* by Steven Connor (1989) p.90).

Whether you read a Warhol piece as a criticism of modernism or simply as a picture of a film star – or as both of these at once – depends on what knowledge and experience you bring to it. Against the modernist notion that art is capable of defining itself, Warhol's impure plural coding recognises that the meanings of art (in fact, the *definition* of art) depend on where it is seen, who sees it, and what mental tools they use in order to read it.

Postmodern art like Warhol's can also be seen as recognising the fact that being an artist does not involve *only* being an artist. The art world perhaps offers artists a particular lifestyle choice, but this does not operate to the exclusion of all other options. Social life today offers a range of different roles and functions, and art is just one of these. Artists do not spend all of their time in an autonomous bubble, breathing in nothing but art. They spend as much time as anyone else going to the cinema, shopping, playing computer games, reading magazines, and watching TV. In other words, artists (and critics) are consumers too. The issue for postmodernists is to explore the points at which these various cultural activities contradict, feed into, and merge with art. Thus postmodernism, rather than abandoning art in favour of mass culture or mass culture in favour of art, suggests that artists and their audiences occupy a slippery position between different 'cultural spaces' (the art world, the shops, the home, different social classes). Postmodern plural coding can therefore be seen as testing or playing with the boundaries.

The end of the art world as they know it?

With postmodernism there are no firm rules which can define for us exactly what the limits, purpose and status of art are. Few attempt to create universal authoritative standards through which to measure artistic quality, and art appears to have become just another consumer choice.

Some critics have therefore lamented postmodernist developments as a decline in values. The American critic Suzi Gablik has argued that contemporary art no longer has a sense of personal commitment or moral authority. According to her, modernism aimed to bring about the spiritual rejuvenation of the western world by being uncompromisingly opposed to material values. Postmodernism, on the other hand, is fatally attracted to commerce, mass culture, and the assembly-line mentality (Warhol called his studio 'The Factory'). From this point of view, modern day mass culture is corrupt because it is an instrument of capitalism, and art's job is to oppose it. But with postmodernism, art has been pulled down from its position of spiritual purity and sucked into the orbit of media, advertising and the *fetishisation of commodities*. So opposition to the system is no longer possible. Thus the difference between modernism and postmodernism is that between serious, spiritual art with a moral centre and floppy, rootless art which commercialism has drained of meaning and emotional force.

Related but somewhat more nuanced objections to postmodernist art have been raised by the American Marxist critic Fredric Jameson. He has argued that the value of modernist painting lay in its ability to express the alienation, fragmentation and isolation of life brought about by modern society. He refers to a well known painting, *The Scream* by Edvard Munch, as a classic example of how modernism uses these themes as part of an adversary stance towards the modern world. Jameson claims that modernism was always informed by the desire to bring about a better world.

As in modernist architecture's utopian schemes, 'great' modernist painting was engaged in a search for new ways of living. Postmodernism has abandoned this project. High and commercial culture have collapsed into each other to such an extent that art cannot find a clear position from which to make powerful critical statements about society: there is no longer any real difference between art and advertising.

Postmodernism: politically weak?

Jameson and others see postmodernism as politically impotent: it refuses to envision an alternative, better way of living, it accepts the way things are, it colludes in, rather than opposes, the status quo. The question of whether postmodernist art is *critical/progressive* or *collusive/regressive* has been much debated. Some critics have sought an answer by trying to separate 'good' from 'bad' postmodernisms.

Examples of the wrangling which can take place over which kind of postmodernism is good and which is bad can be found in the work of a number of critics who publish in the American art journal *October*. Putting it crudely, the *October* critics tend to split postmodernism in the following way:

Weak postmodernism

Straight, old-fashioned painting on canvas. This is seen as merely backwards looking. It repeats old habits of thought, it ignores the contemporary world, it criticises neither high nor mainstream culture; and it is all too clearly aimed at wealthy collectors (painting is still the most saleable art form).

Strong postmodernism

Photography/media based art has more critical potential because it intervenes in mass media images and styles of representation. The mass media is seen to be an image bank full of repressive stereotypes and capitalist ideology. Strong postmodernism subverts the languages of media and consumer society, and at the same time criticises the complacency of the bourgeois art world.

So for the *October* writers, as for Jameson, the question hinges on whether postmodern art from pop onwards celebrates the capitalist state or criticises it.

In addressing these issues, the *October* writers look for points of connection and separation between postmodernist art and older radical art traditions.

Their art belongs to Dada

Throughout the earlier part of the twentieth century, a number of alternative movements had set themselves up, like Warhol's postmodernism, in opposition to puritanical, navel-gazing art-for-art's sake. Of particular importance in this respect are a number of art movements active between roughly 1910 and 1925. Dada, especially, is often seen as the original prototype of how art should go about the business of being radical. A noisy, miscellaneous collection of artists out to annoy the middle classes of Europe and New York in the shadow of the First World War, Dada employed a number of tactics to disrupt bourgeois fantasies about art. Most prominent of these methods was the use of 'found' materials not conventionally associated with fine art. They took materials from the gutter, images from mass culture, and styles of presentation from shop window displays.

Most famous of all, Marcel Duchamp exhibited signed *Readymades* – a urinal, a bottle rack, a comb, etc. – and eventually got them called art (or *anti-art*). For the *October* group and others, such Dadaist strategies were meant as a criticism of the rarefied, stuffy world of high art. The *October* group tended to argue that Dadaist tactics:

- draw attention to the fact that modern capitalist society has turned art into just another set of consumer goods . . .

- parody modern art's uselessness. A urinal exhibited upside-down in an art gallery is fairly detached from its normal function. In the same way, modernism has removed art from everyday life. Readymades satirise the fact that art no longer *does* anything for anybody . . .

- ridicule the high value placed on paintings and sculptures . . .

- show that art is a *social* and not a *natural* category. It is the art world itself – and the social class it is a part of – which allows some things to be called art and some not . . .

- push art off its pedestal . . .

Like Greenberg's modernism, Dada is a form of art which reflects on itself, but unlike this 'pure' modernism, Dadaists insist on remaining firmly within the concrete, material context of everyday activities. Dada can be seen as the start of a long line of art that assaults art, and that attempts to reconcile art and everyday life.

Postmodernism since Pop Art echoes many aspects of Dada. Both challenge the idea that art is autonomous, and both derive images and objects from mass culture. However, the *October* writers are often taxed by the question of whether postmodernism is a continuation or a sell out of this oppositional tradition. They still are not sure whether postmodern art celebrates or criticises mass culture. They point out that the shock tactics of Dada have been institutionalised by museums which collect Dada pieces as though were now 'authentic' art (something which Dada never wanted to be). They also look with dismay at the willingness of artists since Pop to embrace the market. For some critics, Dada has been transformed from a vital, radical tradition into just another old style to be cannibalised by a postmodern art world stuck for ideas, and many conclude that all art can achieve today is the impotent imitation of radical gestures: the art market can absorb and defuse everything, and mass culture turns all art into either an amusing side show or a source of imagery for commercials. From this point of view, postmodernism is just a case of exhaustion, disillusionment, and the abandonment of political motivation.

Further reading

Books which usefully cover aspects of these debates include:

Art in the Age of Mass Media by John A. Walker (1983)
After the Great Divide: Modernism, Mass Culture and Postmodernity by Andreas Huyssen (1986)

A criticism of the criticism

One of the assumptions of Jameson and the *October* critics is that it is not possible for art to be a valuable commodity and an expression of social criticism at the same time. It has to be either one or the other. This black-and-white approach is often more reductive than the art in question. It tries to restrict particular artists to single interpretations in a way which the art itself (at least as we have been describing it in this chapter) refuses to do. The Dada artist Hans Richter noted that 'it was . . . conventional yes/no thinking that Dada was trying to blow sky high', and what we have been calling the *between-ness* and *plural coding* of postmodernist art similarly refuses to let itself be pinned to a single interpretation. It is sometimes pointed out that postmodernism replaces *either/or* thinking with *both/and* thinking.

Postmodern art like Warhol's, instead of opting for one level of cultural activity and against another, adopts a complex position of betweenness, *border tension* or *fringe interference*:

❝ postmodernism's distinctive character lies in this . . . wholesale 'nudging' commitment to doubleness, or duplicity ❞

The Politics of Postmodernism by Linda Hutcheon, (1989) p.1

In other words, postmodernist artists can be both critical *and* celebratory of the mass culture which many (modernist) critics want art to simply condemn. They can similarly criticise the art institution at the same time as they exploit it.

Summary

Postmodernist art forms

- aim to appeal to a wider audience
- take issue with the idea that art occupies a special area fenced off from the rest of social life
- re-think the relationship between art and popular culture, and reconsider the supposed differences between works of art and other consumer goods
- are against modernism's idea that art defines itself, and see the 'artness' of objects and images as defined by social acts of interpretation
- propose that all cultural production is involved in complex social relations. Artists are very much *inside* society. Whereas the critical vs. conservative debate assumes that artists have to be in a position *outside* of popular culture and commodification in order to offer a substantial critique of them, postmodernism suggests that such a position might be neither possible nor desirable
- do not define themselves by rejecting either modernism or popular culture, but exist as an unsteady territory between the two.

A final thought

A modernist view: an artist, starving in his garret, gets inspiration from popular culture for his latest masterpiece, which then goes on to outrage the academy.

A postmodernist view: contemporary British art star Damien Hirst makes a jaunty promotional video for the group *Blur*, complete with starlets from the British soft pornography industry, and doesn't outrage anybody.

4
THE TROUBLE WITH REALITY

It is sometimes said that theories of postmodernism proclaim 'the end of the real'. While this may be something of an exaggeration, it is true to say that many of these theories do set out to raise doubts about the relationship between reality and representation. The claim here is not quite that nothing is real, but that there is no simple, direct relationship between reality and its supposed expression in words and pictures.

Within theories of postmodernism, these questions are sometimes addressed to relatively recent developments in mass communications and the electronic reproduction of sound, image and text. Television has often been central in this area. This is not to say that television is to blame for producing postmodern conditions, or that it has single-handedly given us a problem with reality. It is rather that television has often served as a kind of emblem of the issues which theorists of postmodernism try to describe.

In this chapter we will look at a few of the ways television has been used in postmodernist theory and consider in detail the arguments that some postmodern theory puts forward about the problematic relationship between reality and image in contemporary culture. In doing this we will examine some of the propositions put forward by the French theorist Jean Baudrillard (born 1929).

On Television

Television has been an object of academic enquiry and controversy since long before the concerns of postmodernism gained currency. There have been many approaches to scholarly analysis of TV. One such trend was concerned with the effects that TV might have on the cultural 'health' of the population. In the 1950s and 1960s, especially, many critics were worried that TV (and other popular forms from paperback novels to rock 'n' roll) posed a threat to both the folk heritage of 'the people', and the high arts. More recent enquiries into the uses and pleasures of popular media have attacked the arguably elitist and patronising tone of earlier work in this area.

In another tradition, innumerable psychologists and sociologists have tried to assess the impact of TV on the psychology and behaviour of its viewers, particularly children and adolescents. On-going research into these supposed effects has proved highly ambivalent at best, with wildly inconsistent results being reported by different projects.

Neither of these more orthodox attempts to offer a definitive description of the social and aesthetic implications of TV have so far succeeded in providing a complete picture of the area. It has proved hard for theorists to account for TV in its entirety, or at least to provide a single, fully satisfactory analytical model. Even within the apparently small world of postmodern theory, there is still little consensus about how best to describe its meanings and functions. This is partly due to the sheer variety of its output, which makes it hard to find any single factor which is common to all products of TV. Another problem is that no researcher can know of all the different audiences for any one programme, or of how they might (or might not) respond to it. Despite (and in some cases because of) its resistance to simplification or generalisation, TV is sometimes seen as one of the clearest embodiments of postmodernism, and there are several reasons for this.

On one level it can be argued that the medium of TV is postmodern because it seems radically different from some of the main principles behind modernist art. From this perspective, attention might focus on the formal qualities of TV, and on aspects of TV's general dynamics. These might include the way it uses sounds and images, the experience of TV as a constant turnover of images, and the ability of viewers to zap from one channel to another.

On another level, TV is of interest to theorists of postmodernism because it is thought to be a key example of important expansions in what is sometimes called *consumer culture*. From this viewpoint, TV is examined in terms of its relation to the industrial, economic and technological developments of 'advanced' society. As well as looking at the economic and industrial links of TV to the growth of a new global mass culture, some approaches focus on the content of specific programmes by looking at how particular stories reflect postmodern social conditions.

Finally, TV is of great importance to researchers who consider themselves to be offering postmodernist accounts of popular culture. From this perspective, both aesthetic and social/political aspects of TV are considered, but the interest lies more in how to look at popular culture in a way which departs from earlier critical approaches. It is claimed that these earlier, modernist approaches (as we saw in Chapter 2) maintained a clear-cut and elitist distinction between high and mass culture. A new, postmodernist model of culture is therefore required.

Of course, the angles on TV I have identified above overlap in all sorts of ways. For instance, its visual styles may be linked in complex ways to its industrial and economic attachments. And this in turn is one of the issues addressed by theorists and researchers who wish to question the established modernist approach to cultural criticism.

TV as postmodern art form?

For the sake of clarity, some of the differences between artistic modernism and postmodern TV have been divided below into the categories of *production*, *exhibition*, and *reception*.

Style of production

To put it crudely, modernist, romantic ideas about art stressed the creativity of the individual genius, who was valued for struggling to express her or his unique emotions and insights in material such as paint. With the emphasis very much on the singularity of the artist it follows that modernism also valued the physical qualities of the individual work of art itself, and associated these qualities – present in brush-strokes, chisel marks, idiosyncratic stylistic quirks, and so on –

with notions like 'integrity', 'authenticity' and 'originality'. Putting aside the question of whether these are really adequate ways of looking at art, it should become clear that they do not necessarily apply very comfortably to TV.

Unlike most works of art, a TV programme has no individual creator. Despite the possible talents of particular celebrities, script-writers, and so forth, that go into the making of a programme, and although certain directors do have recognisable styles, the final product is nearly always such a team effort that no single person can be said to have created it. Before our TV receivers pick the transmission up, the programme has been touched by a whole network of personnel, who, even if they have not directly influenced the content of the broadcast, have had some responsibility in making it happen. Hence the way TV is made does not conform to conventional notions of handicraft, or to the familiar picture of the genius pouring his or her innermost thoughts into his or her own work of art.

Style of exhibition

We tend to think of paintings and sculptures as being viewed in relatively exclusive spaces like galleries and museums. Some writers (notably the sociologist Pierre Bourdieu) have examined how these spaces are often organised in a way that encourages specific, modernist notions of what art is and how to look at it. In the first place, it is argued, the selection and showing of certain objects by galleries and museums instantly loads these objects with cultural baggage: it confers the status of art upon them. But, beyond that, the way art is generally exhibited (and discussed) promotes the modernist idea that works of art exist in a naturally special realm of experience independent of the rest of life. Works of art are traditionally meant to be experienced at first hand by a specific, restricted audience in a specially designed high culture environment. TV is, by virtue of its style of exhibition, in stark contrast to this.

We have suggested that TV programmes are created by a long chain of personnel, rather than by a single creative being. Similarly, although each programme is made only once, it can always make a potentially infinite number of appearances on a potentially infinite number of screens. While most paintings and sculptures are intended to exist as one-offs, each broadcast TV programme can therefore be said to have *multiplicity* built into it. On the one hand it may be endlessly copied, saved, exchanged, and re-shown any number of times on video tapes around the world. To this extent TV broadcasts are a kind of art which can theoretically be owned by everyone. One the other hand, each programme is transmitted to millions of 'sites' at once and (much like information on the internet) is in a sense free of fixed location.

Styles of reception

In the case of traditional fine art, both the architecture of the exhibition space itself and the codes of behaviour supposedly proper to the art world seem designed to encourage a private, one-to-one relationship between the viewer and the work of art. The presentation of the art work in a pristine, often white room contributes to the feeling that each piece should be attended to on its own terms, uncontaminated by either neighbouring works of art or the outside world. Reception of the art work, then, often takes place in a hushed, reverential atmosphere in which each piece apparently demands of the visitor a special aesthetic kind of contemplation. In these ways it is possible to see the viewing of art as a somewhat *regulated* activity.

If art is conventionally confined to very particular sites and therefore to fairly specific audiences, TV is virtually the opposite: it is a mass medium watched in familiar spaces (the home, the pub, the Chinese take-away, the classroom) by a potentially unlimited audience. There are almost as many different places in which TV can be shown as there are TV sets in the world. And there are almost as many ways of using it. There are, theoretically at least, no restrictions on where it can be shown, who can watch it, or how it should be watched. Unlike the consumption of art there is – again in theory – no established social code or etiquette regarding appropriate viewing behaviour.

Where the field of modernist painting and sculpture thrives on the idea that its objects require a protracted, intent, somehow pure aesthetic gaze, TV programmes can either be gazed at in fascination, glanced at distractedly while you are doing something else, left switched on while you are in another room, sworn at or argued with, turned up to drown another noise out, or watched for entertainment or education. You can also throw things at them, and zap between them. So although schedulers and advertisers might like to imagine you in thrall to the box, it is far more likely that you use it in a variety of ways for various purposes, and that you fairly often ignore it. The consumption of TV is, then, comparatively *unregulated* and unpredictable.

As has already been suggested, one of the ways in which TV is used as a source for the creation of private video tape archives. In this way, we can 'possess' particular programmes, and in doing so make permanent the otherwise transient moment in what is sometimes called TV's flow of sounds and images. Unless the consumer decides to store certain broadcasts on tape – perhaps frequently re-viewing them, perhaps pausing on favourite instants, and in the process making them into very different kinds of objects – the TV programme has a fleeting existence which distinguishes it from what we might think of as the traditional relationship between art and 'timelessness'.

Ways of watching TV: an open and closed case

Modernist theories of art fostered the impression that a work of art can and should be experienced in its own right, on its own terms, and for its own sake, without reference to other objects in the world. The familiar presentation of modern art works against supposedly neutral white walls is intended to promote this idea. They are regularly presented as though they are permanent, timeless artefacts, requiring no external justification or explanation, and free of any 'outside' influence. The art works are somehow meant to emit a sense of their own presence. But on TV, individual programmes and images are not isolated against, or surrounded by, some polite, neutral ground. Instead they seem to fight for our attention in a crowded – some would say feverish or superficial, others would say exhilarating – environment in which representations proliferate and bounce off each other. They cannot, then, be easily characterised in terms of aesthetic purity or self-sufficiency.

An interesting case is that of the soap opera. Unlike most novels, which tend to be structured around the build-up to how they are going to end, soaps tend to present on-going stories that have no end in sight. They can go on for years, sometimes seeming to be made up as they go along, the interrelationships in their story lines constantly gathering ever greater degrees of intricacy. Single plot developments naturally reach conclusions of sorts, but in the world of the soap, the case is never really closed. New details about its fictional past are forever coming to light, cats get let out of bags, long forgotten characters keep returning to disrupt the present, and old plot-lines are continually re-visited, revised and milked for new twists. In this world, each episode is affected by the episodes which have gone before it, and contains the seeds of numerous new developments to come. A single event in one programme can have repercussions that affect years of unfolding narrative, yet the lead-up to that single event can be traced back through an endless chain of preceding, often seemingly insignificant incidents. In a sense the separate episodes bleed into each other so that the open-ended series is a continuum in which, unlike many conventional works of art, no individual instalment wants to be seen as a complete, self-enclosed entity.

So although in one way many soaps often seem to be trapped in their own insular universe, we can see them as an example of the inherently 'open' programme. We can look in similar terms at TV commercials, which are often open in the way that they refer to other media products. Many adverts assume that viewers possess a wide knowledge of popular culture, and play on this knowledge by producing a whole range of quotes, in-jokes, parodies, pastiches and imitations of Hollywood movies, TV programmes and other adverts. In addition, they frequently borrow their soundtracks from any point in the history of popular and classical music, or from world music. Commercials and adverts do not attempt to work independently or be seen as self enclosed wholes, but are explicitly imprinted with – and overtly made out of – their cultural surroundings.

It is possible, then, to draw a picture of TV, and the media in general, in which individual items are in various ways open to each other. But this does not mean that they are correspondingly open to the world. Rather, for some chroniclers of the postmodern, it means that the contemporary mediascape is more like a closed circuit than an open forum. So caught up are the products of the media in chatting among themselves that they have effectively shut the world out.

This is the situation described by Umberto Eco in his 1984 essay *A Guide to the Neo-Television of the 1980s*. In that short piece, Eco argues that TV is so absorbed in itself that it has now virtually turned its back on the external world. Examples of being so self-absorbed include:

- chat shows
- award ceremonies
- TV news items about TV celebrities
- TV documentaries about the making of TV
- TV quiz shows in which contestants (sometimes TV personalities) are quizzed about TV shows
- TV shows in which the public complain about/praise TV shows
- out-takes shows
- ads which recycle/spoof old ads
- sit-coms self-consciously produced in a style meant to evoke good old fashioned classic comedy
- airing of newly discovered lost episodes of old sit-coms

In this world of what Eco calls *neo-TV*, something being on TV is remarkable or newsworthy in itself. In nature programming, for instance, it is not the mating-procedures of certain animals which are astounding, so much as the fact that they have been captured for the first time on camera. The same goes for candid interviews with members of royalty. The very fact that the royal personage has opened her/his heart on TV can send shock waves around the globe, even when the revelations are utterly banal and predictable (especially when leaked to the press days in advance). And who would be interested in probes which did *not* send back remarkable pictures (digitally enhanced and coloured before being shown on news broadcasts the world over) of unexplored planetary surfaces?

In all of these cases Eco would argue that fascination lies not in what the appearance *refers* to – the heavenly body, the royal personage, the amorous creature – but in the *fact of televisual appearance itself*. And this fascination is not only felt by the audience. As Eco would argue, TV itself is fascinated with, and is forever congratulating itself on, its own productions, its own operation, and its own ability to make history.

A note of caution

All of this begins to give the impression that TV is in a world of its own. Although, as I have suggested, no single item in the media can be seen as an isolated, self-enclosed entity, Eco's image of neo-TV talking to itself does involve taking a detached overview of TV in general and seeing it as in a sense abstract and liberated from outside influence. In this way, some postmodern accounts of TV represent it as more whole or unified than is probably the case.

— Welcome to Planet Baudrillard —

Umberto Eco saw the world of neo-TV as so turned in upon itself that there was little space left for the real world. Jean Baudrillard (1929–) has similarly described media culture as consumed by what he calls 'an effect of frantic self-referentiality', but he has gone much further than Eco in exploring the implications of this effect. As well as the media now operating without having to make any necessary reference to reality, we now face a situation in which, to Baudrillard's mind, the image 'bears no relation to any reality whatever: it is its own pure simulacrum.' (*Selected Writings*, 1988 p.170).

Baudrillard has been one of the key figures in the postmodernism debate. Most surveys of the subject take his work to be of central importance, and a number of theorists have taken up and adapted his ideas. Although he has actually used the term postmodern only sparingly, his work is often seen to provide especially pungent, if mind-bending, descriptions of the brave new world of postmodern society. Responses to many of his books and essays, particularly since the late 1970s, have ranged from outrage and bewilderment to uncritical enthusiasm. He has been seen as a weaver of fascinating, elusive texts which play with the (non) meanings of a world engulfed by media. And he has been seen as an infuriating apologist for just about everything that some see as bad about the media and the society that spawned them. In the following reading of Baudrillard we will touch on just part of the work he has done since his first published book, *The System of Objects* (1968).

It is often said that wherever you look, there are pictures. Tee-shirts, billboards, posters, packaging, newspapers, magazines, TV, cinema, computers and video games can all be listed as sources of imagery. Many of us also own cameras and camcorders, and most of us are regularly recorded, however unknowingly, by closed circuit surveillance cameras in shops and high streets. Some proud parents now video their children being born, and many foetuses now put in an early screen preview. For Baudrillard, this apparent obsession with images has fundamentally altered our world.

On its simplest level, Baudrillard's work suggests that all this representation has saturated reality to such an extent that experience can only take place at a remove. We can experience the world only through a kind of filter of preconceptions and expectations fabricated in advance by a culture swamped by images. How, Baudrillard might ask, can you visit, or even live in, New York City without that experience being informed by all the New York Cities you know from movies and TV shows? Or how can you even express your love for someone without that expression recalling in some way the innumerable soaps and films in which the vicissitudes of love are played out daily? Indeed, would those 'three little words' be so emotionally weighted – would you even feel the same desire to utter them upon occasion – had you *not* seen and heard them uttered a million times before?

But Baudrillard's writings do offer much more than the simple study of media effects. He has looked at a wide range of cultural phenomena from all aspects of contemporary existence and much of his work, rather than occupying any one discipline or school of thought, is best seen as a sort of meeting place for linguistics, sociology, philosophy, political theory and science fiction. The analysis of TV and film, although playing an important part in Baudrillard's work, is therefore just one aspect of his theorisation of the postmodern situation.

This situation appears in Baudrillard's work in several guises, and he likes to give it funky yet apocalyptic sounding names like 'hyperreality', 'implosion', 'cyberblitz' and 'the code'. All of these have fairly different connotations, and their meanings do shift and change throughout Baudrillard's work, but they are all closely related to what Baudrillard calls *simulation*. Features of contemporary life as apparently diverse as fashion, environmental design, opinion polls, theme parks, telecommunications and cybernetics have all been rolled together in Baudrillard's hands as manifestations of the single, shiny new regime of simulation. Baudrillard uses this term in a bewildering variety of ways, but often seems to mean by it little more than a generalised realm of reproductions, images, representations and models. For example, in his 1981 book *Simulations*, Disneyland, psychosomatic illness, the Watergate scandal and hijacks are all given the same Baudrillard treatment.

Dictionaries link simulation to the fake, the counterfeit, and the inauthentic. Baudrillard retains these meanings to a certain extent, but pushes them considerably further, so that simulation can no longer be seen clearly as the opposite of truth. We might naturally assume that simulation either duplicates or is emitted by a pre-given real. In this sense we might think that simulation and reality have a necessary attachment to each other. But for Baudrillard, this connection has long since snapped, so that simulation can no longer be taken as either an imitation or distortion of reality, or as a copy of an original. In Baudrillard's dizzying cosmos there is no firm, pure reality left against which we can measure the truth or falsity of a representation, and electronic reproduction has gone so far that the notion of originality is (or ought to be) irrelevant.

Computer-generated images and spaces are the most obvious example of this. They have their own sense of reality (what is sometimes called 'telepresence') which does not depend on the existence of anything outside of their virtual world. One critic, Michael Heim, has noted that 'virtual entities are not representations. They do not re-present. They do not present again something that is already present somewhere else' (*Cyberspace/Cyberbodies/Cyberpunk*, edited by Featherstone and Burrows, 1995). Although Heim makes no reference to him, this description is close to Baudrillard's definition of simulation as 'the generation of models of a real without origin or reality'. But you do not have to sit at a computer all day, wear virtual reality goggles, or even watch a multimillion dollar special effects extravaganza at your local multiplex in order to find simulation at work. Simulation is for Baudrillard a widespread cultural condition and not an 'event' restricted to a particular technology. We have entered a state of affairs in which, as Baudrillard says, 'it is now a principle of simulation, and not of reality, that regulates all of social life' (*Selected Writings* 1988, p.120).

—— Images in the floating world ——

In a lecture called *The Evil Demon of Images*, presented at the

University of Sydney in 1987, and published as a booklet in 1988, Baudrillard declared that:

❝ It is the reference principle of images which must be doubted, this strategy by means of which they always appear to refer to a real world, to real objects, and to reproduce something which is logically, and chronologically, anterior to themselves. None of this is true . . . images precede the real to the extent that they invert the causal and logical order of the real and its reproduction. ❞

(page 13)

As you can tell, the position that Baudrillard takes can sometimes seem baffling and rather extreme. We can begin to make sense of it by breaking down the above statement into its two main propositions, and spending some time considering each in detail.

Baudrillard's first proposition: the reference principle of images must be doubted

This carries on from what we have suggested about neo-TV. For Baudrillard, the media not only talk among themselves (as they did for Eco) but are a kind of virtual collage of free-floating images which have cut themselves loose from the burden of having to represent anything other than themselves. In Baudrillard's scheme of things, representation is now on automatic pilot. In its own orbit, representation can now operate without ever having to land on the apparently solid ground of facts, reality or history. Consider three examples which might be said to bring the reference principle into doubt:

You are watching on a videotape of a contemporary film an image of a woman smoking a cigarette. She looks cool, seductive, and fairly dangerous. Her smoking gives her this sort of aura. There is something about the way she lights her cigarette . . . you find this an attractive image. Perhaps you would quite like to look like that yourself. Has any of this to do with the actuality of smouldering tobacco? Or is it intimately connected to all the other cinematic femmes fatales you have seen light up before? Is it in fact the smoking itself, or the very 'film-ness' of the image which entices you?

You read *The National Enquirer*, an American tabloid with international circulation. Front page headlines for August 6 1996 tell you that 'Jacko's nose drops off'. Wherein lies the reality, or the meaning, to which this paper refers? Who is Jacko, really? What do we really know about him? What is the relation between the him we do know and the real him? How many of the rumours about him are true, and how many false? Does this distinction matter any longer? Are the rumours, regardless of their truth or falsity, separable from who we think of as Jacko? Are the representations of Jacko determined in any way by the qualities of the actual person they seem to refer to, or are they produced by the effect which constant representation itself has generated? In other words, is Jacko himself a simulation?

You wear expensive brand-name sneakers and tracksuits for their fashionability, but you have no interest in sports. What 'underlying reality' do your clothes and footwear refer to? Is there any sense in trying to rationalise or explain fashion, or search for a hidden cause of which this particular fashion is the effect? Is the pricetag on your sneakers determined by anything more concrete than the image of the brand name? What reality does the brand name represent other than its own?

What Baudrillard would see in all of these cases is a situation in which representations, broadly defined, are no longer determined by an essential connection to the things which they are supposed to represent.

Other commentators have agreed with Baudrillard in this respect. In his 1992 book, *Postmodernism, or the Cultural Logic of Late Capitalism* (expanded from some essays first published in the 1980s), the American critic Fredric Jameson makes a similar point regarding what he sees as the 'depthlessness' of contemporary cultural production. Jameson identifies postmodern 'formal features' in art, architecture, film, video and TV, and finds in them only a superficial cutting and pasting of ready made images and styles. These are seen by Jameson as signs abstracted from their true origins and re-used in meaningless new combinations in the trivial, commercialised space created by mass culture. Unlike Baudrillard, Jameson makes little attempt to hide his disgust at the shallowness of postmodern artefacts. To illustrate his point he contrasts two famous pictures of footwear. First, he looks at a painting by Vincent Van Gogh called *Peasant Shoes*. This painting is seen by Jameson as a deep, modernist one. The very substance of the lumps and furrows of encrusted oil paint somehow offer themselves up as recordings of an authentic world of rural poverty and agricultural misery. The painting is, for Jameson, firmly embedded in a specific social, geographical, historical and personal situation, and as such deserves its status as one of the great 'canonical works of high modernism.'

On the other hand, he looks at *Diamond Dust Shoes* by Andy Warhol. Unlike the Van Gogh painting, claims Jameson, it is impossible to read anything of significance into Warhol's work. Whereas the truth of *Peasant Shoes* lies in the way Jameson can read into it the whole brutal world of peasant toil, the Warhol piece merely presents itself as a blank surface. This is partly because, as a photographically derived screen print, it is literally flat and more or less mechanical. Thus it is difficult for Jameson to read it in terms of personal expression. Another problem is that it presents the images of shoes as 'shorn of their earlier life-world'. That is to say, they simply float decoratively, placed in no particular setting. They are, in fact, pure images, in the sense that they are derived not from reality, as was the case with Van Gogh (or so Jameson supposes), but from other images. Warhol has not observed an actual pair of shoes and attempted to express through them the real way of life of which they are a part. Instead he has merely duplicated what Jameson calls the debased, depthless appearance of the glossy advertising image.

This is just one of the examples Jameson gives as symptomatic of our current social condition in which 'depth is replaced by surface'. Another writer who has expressed similar concerns is Dick Hebdige, particularly in his book *Hiding in the Light* (1988). Rather as Jameson set up two paintings in opposition to each other – one to represent the authentic old world, the other to symbolise the superficial new world – Hebdige takes two contemporary magazines, and proposes that a huge chasm separates their respective attitudes. On one side of this chasm he places a periodical called *Ten.8*, a 'serious' photography magazine with an emphasis on theory and politics, read mainly by the academic market. On the other side, he places *The Face,* perhaps the definitive, and certainly the most influential, British style magazine of the 1980s.

Hebdige sees *Ten.8* as representative of an older, graver attitude to images. In its pages writers on photography analyse images in terms of their theoretical frameworks, political implications and historical backgrounds. In this journal, words are used to ground, situate and tame images. Images are seen as in need of explanation.

Meanwhile *The Face* lets images have the upper hand. Instead of trying to pin pictures down or solve them, it sets them loose from what Hebdige calls 'the constraints imposed by the rationalist theology of representation'. In other words, *The Face* uses images for their style value rather than for some notion of their deep meaning. Unlike *Ten.8*, *The Face* and its readership do not really care where an image comes from or what it says. All that matters is the effect (Jameson calls this the *intensity* as opposed to the *meaning*) of an image *as an image*.

As you will have gathered, the traits identified by Jameson and Hebdige are by no means restricted to a single art form. In the realm of moving images alone many critics have found similar qualities in rock videos, advertising campaigns, TV programmes like *Miami Vice*, and films like *Blue Velvet*. A more recent example would be Quentin Tarantino's *Pulp Fiction* (1994). In this film, we get no sense that Tarantino is trying to portray a real world. We suspect that he knows little about the criminal underworld which the film seems to portray and that he is dealing almost entirely in cinematic signs, quotes, and clichés. Yet whether or not you 'get the references' is as irrelevant as which particular songs dance records get their samples from. In Tarantino's film we are not invited to be outraged by acts of violence, and critical responses to the film have tended to shy away from discussing the racist, sexist and homophobic representations in Tarantino's work. The reason for this is that the film seems to put everything in cinematic quotation marks. We hardly take it as showing anything other than a celluloid film world. It makes no attempt at revealing to us how things really are: it is purely about its own intensity, its own effect as a piece of fictional film. The title itself (as it had in the Tarantino-scripted *True Romance*) signals that it is not to be taken too seriously. Like all of the examples touched on above, *Pulp Fiction* is a case of what Baudrillard calls 'the emancipation of the sign . . . from any archaic obligation it might have to designate something' (*Selected Writings*, 1988 p.125). To try and figure out what it is 'really' all about is to look almost stuffy and old fashioned.

So what we are presented with in the postmodern mediascape is a matter of circulating surfaces: a zone in which signs can function without having to be plugged in to what we might think of as a fundamental, authentic realm of existence. What we have, says Jean Baudrillard, is a *centreless network of communication* which endlessly reproduces and cannibalises its own constant production of simulations, a situation in which the image is a 'phantasm of authenticity which always ends up just short of reality' (*The Revenge of the Crystal*, 1990).

Baudrillard's second Proposition: Images precede the real to the extent that they invert the causal and logical order of the real and its reproduction

The big paradox in Baudrillard's work is that, while simulations are emancipated from any reference to reality, they are nevertheless firmly embedded in our lives. They may not refer to some natural, unsimulated reality, but they do have very real effects. In the course of one day we might cry along with a weepie, feel thirsty when looking at an advert for beer, have our faith in human nature shaken by the news, be scared silly by a slasher movie, get excited by seeing a celebrity in the street . . . in these ways we might say that far from being detached in their own little world, simulations are deeply connected to real life.

Baudrillard would not necessarily disagree with this point, but he might draw quite surprising conclusions from it. He would suggest something along the following lines:

- Yes, life is full of simulations, but . . .

- this only shows that reality has become confused with empty, hollow signs!

- Yes, you could argue that because simulations have certain actual effects on people they are therefore real, but . . .

- you've got it the wrong way around: simulation is real only to the extent that reality is already simulated!

- Yes, this does in a sense show that simulations make reference to things, but . . .

- given that reality is always already simulated, reference can only be to simulation and not to some pure, unadulterated reality!

This is only a crude caricature of Baudrillard's subtle and evasive writing, but it does at least give an impression of the twisted logic which infests it, and which he says characterises our current 'regime'.

In Baudrillard-land, the distinction between simulation and reality has collapsed. In *The Evil Demon of Images*, he calls this a telescoping or implosion of image into reality. We hinted at some of the ways in which this has happened when we noted how images intersect with (and, we might add, enable) certain experiences of the world. It will not surprise you to learn that Baudrillard goes a lot further than this simple observation. In fact, he turns conventional thinking about the 'logical order of the real and its reproduction' inside out, so that images do not just intersect with the real; they precede it, anticipate it, absorb it, and produce it. Even with the examples given above, Baudrillard would claim that reality was an 'effect' of representation. He makes this point rather dramatically in a passage from his travelogue, *America* (1988, first published in France 1986):

> ❢ Everything is destined to reappear as simulation. Landscapes as photography, women as the sexual scenario, thoughts as writing, terrorism as fashion and the media. Things seem only to exist by virtue of this strange destiny. You wonder whether the world itself isn't just here to serve as advertising copy in some other world. ❢ (page 32)

Some examples

You turn on a fly-on-the-wall TV documentary which follows events in the day-to-day life of a typical family. It seems to bear all the marks of authenticity: there is no sense in which we think of the family as actors. These are real people, after all, and we are watching reality unfold in real time, though only as real life soap. Their lives seem full of incident, and there are some juicy, pretty heated rows. But then you wonder (as though it makes any difference): to what extent are they playing up to the recording equipment? If you were not there to watch, would there be anything worth watching? Suddenly suspicious of the whole fly-on-the-wall concept, you switch over to the news. It's a live on-the-spot report from the site of a large urban disturbance. A reporter stands before a debris-strewn street and reports, with just the slightest hint of disappointment, that all is quiet for the moment. Prompted by our henchman in the studio, she notes – a little ominously, but also perhaps a little hopefully – that there are fears that violence might flare up again later tonight. Needless to say, her prediction proves right. Had the rioters watched the news? Are they putting on a show for the cameras?

As Baudrillard asks in *The Evil Demon of Images*: 'What else does the media dream of if not raising up events by its very presence?' (page 22).

You are casting your vote in a general election. Is your vote based on some idea of real politics, or is it informed by the endless soundbites, PR exercises, photo calls, image contests and smug grins which make up the political arena today? Can you think of politics in separation from the media? Is there any distinction to be made between real (deep) and unreal (shallow) politics? In this example, we could say that image and reality are totally intertwined: notions of true versus false hardly come into the equation. If this seems controversial, consider the cases of the weepie and pornography instead. Does it make any sense at all to distinguish between genuine emotions, and the tears produced by sentimental cinema? Is there any real difference between 'natural' sexuality and the desires and pleasures provoked, encouraged, and confirmed by mass-produced pornography?

In all of these cases, genuine and artificial have overlapped.

When you go food shopping you choose between designer foods, health foods, exotic foods, slim-line foods, sinful foods, luxury foods, natural foods, traditional foods, homemade foods, convenience foods, and 'TV dinners'. Some foods (especially desserts) are 'as good as granny used to make'. Others (especially junk food) are 'chip shop style' or 'American style'. Is food now ever just food, or is it always attached to a style, a lifestyle, a body image or a social type? Perhaps you base your food buying decisions on the kind of person you see yourself as. But where did you get this image from? Can you separate it from the various identities you are sold daily in advertising, fashion/lifestyle/interior decoration magazines, sex technique videos, shop window displays, fitness programmes, pop records? Do you have any reason to suppose that the kind of person you are, or could become, is not a fulfilment of pre-existing models of thought and behaviour? Are you really anything more than a type?

All of these examples demonstrate how (as Baudrillard would see it) the line between simulation and reality has been erased. As Baudrillard would say, there is no way of identifying a real which exists outside of simulation, because we live in a society which is structured according to all sorts of beliefs, ideals, and blueprints. In short, reality is structured according to codes. Some codes are manifested in directly political ways – in the drafting of bills, the creation and enforcing of laws, and so on. Some are inscribed into concrete institutions – education, industry and prisons, for example. Others appear in less obvious ways – such as entertainment media, consumer goods, architecture and designed environments. Still more show themselves in the constant surveys, polls and questionnaires which classify the population according to their consumption patterns, income brackets, sexual orientations and so forth. None of these codes can rightfully be called natural or timeless, but all can be said to precede the real in the sense that they produce the real social order in which we all participate. And all can be said to feel real in the sense that they affect real people. To quote from Baudrillard's *America*:

> ❦ The only physical beauty is created by plastic surgery, the only urban beauty by landscape surgery, the only opinion by opinion poll surgery . . . and now, with genetic engineering, comes plastic surgery for the whole human species. ❦ (page 32)

And from *Simulations*:

> ❦ It is now impossible to isolate the processes of the real or to prove the real . . . all hold-ups, hijacks and the like are now as it were simulations . . . *inscribed in advance* in the decoding and orchestration rituals of the media. ❦ (pages 41–2)

Because of the way it suggests that the real is an effect of simulation, it would be easy to discuss all of this in terms of how people are affected or manipulated by various cultural influences. We might, for instance, try to fit Baudrillard into a critical tradition which looks at how people are persuaded or encouraged to be the good consumers that the system requires in order to keep itself going. It might be tempting to try and find in Baudrillard proof of the influence of TV on the supposedly impressionable masses. And we might try to find proof of Baudrillard's theories in those people who apparently write to TV actors, believing them to be the characters they portray.

But Baudrillard is keen to distance himself from these kinds of reading of his work. The image of people being manipulated or affected is misleading because it suggests that a gap naturally exists between people and the forces which supposedly shape them. In other words, it suggests that people can exist in an independent, fundamentally unaffected state at some point prior to the system coming along and working on them. In Baudrillard's scheme of things, this is not possible. As far as he is concerned, we are always already caught up in the workings of simulation: 'the social contract has become a pact of simulation, sealed by the media and information', so we are always already part of the network. For Baudrillard, nothing is outside of the flow of signs, codes, and simulations.

How are we to react to this scenario? What impact does it have on the lives we lead and the artefacts we make and use? Baudrillard's answer is that it generates *panic*. We desperately try to get out of simulation by producing events, activities, images and objects which assure us of their (and our) reality. In an attempt to compensate for the fading of the real, we make a fetish of the supposedly authentic. We manufacture an 'escalation of the lived experience . . . a panic-stricken production of the real and the referential.' (Simulations pages 12-13).

Baudrillard calls this the *hyperreal* or more-real-than-real:

- jogging, weight training, aerobics, body-piercing, bungee jumping, white-water rafting, adventure holidays

- private life going public in talk shows, true-life stories, tabloid exposés, autobiographies

- interactive TV, phone-in surveys, courtroom TV, TV vérité, car crash/execution/surgery videos

- CDs with the built-in scratch of records, John Lennon's tinny voice on a 'new' Beatles single, groups unplugged on MTV, live recordings

- giant video screens bringing you closer to the event at stadium concerts, sports venues, party conferences

- digital special effects, surround-sound, virtual reality

- songs, ads and self-help manuals which implore you to find yourself, be yourself, do it your way, express yourself, unlock the real you, find your inner child

You could add plenty more examples of your own to this list. They all illustrate Baudrillard's claim that 'when the real is no longer what it used to be, nostalgia assumes its full meaning. There is a proliferation of myths of origin and signs of reality; of second-hand truth, objectivity and authenticity' (*Simulations*, page 12). That is, they all attempt to deter, or provide alibis for, the disappearance of the real at the hands of simulation. The Baudrillardian irony, however, is that these attempts to increase the feel of reality are themselves simulations. Their authenticity is a special effect. They are *hyperreal* rather than *really* real.

We *manufacture the real* because of simulation. So once again we find that the real is not so much given as produced. Which basically means that we cannot win. This is why Baudrillard says that 'images precede the real', and this is why the relationship between the real and its representation is now inverted. The logical order of things might be that reality expresses itself through representations, but this has been turned upside down.

In summary

Baudrillard thinks we need to reconsider *what* we mean reality to be, and *where* we consider it to be in relation to its supposed reproduction.

In our 'normal' way of thinking, images and other forms of representation have a lazy relationship to the real: they are subservient to reality. Reality comes first, it is in the driver's seat. Something about reality determines or produces its 'simulation'.

In Baudrillard's way of thinking, reality has a lazy relationship to images and other forms of representation. It is subservient to representation. Reality comes second, it takes the back seat. Something about simulation determines or produces reality.

Influences, comparisons and dialogues

Although Baudrillard's writings do have a recognisably Baudrillardian tone, they actually feed off and develop the ideas of a number of other thinkers. As you will see, his speculations on how simulations have altered the relationship between reality and representation have a lot in common with some of the other postmodern theorists discussed later in this book. His works also show the influence of several thinkers who have developed theories about media culture from within a loosely Marxist framework. As well as being important to Baudrillard, some of them have been influential to the formation of postmodern theory in general. Most provide important touchstones for a lot of the ideas discussed in the rest of this book.

Karl Marx (1818–1883)

The political philosopher Karl Marx provided perhaps the most influential account of modernity. His arguments about the impact of industrialisation and capitalist expansion have helped to shape the work of countless social analysts throughout the twentieth century, and many theories of postmodernism address themselves in one way or another to his ideas. We cannot attempt to do justice to the full scope of Marx's ideas here. But we can note some of the ideas which have informed Baudrillard's outlook on postmodern culture.

At the time when Marx was writing, modern industry was in a constant search for new sources of labour, new raw materials, new technologies, and new ways of spreading into social life. Marx looked at this, but recognised in it a potential for improving the material comforts of people's lives. Modernity was far from all bad: it had a great capacity for improving people's standards of living. Yet Marx also recognised that the innovations of modernity were propelled by the capitalist economic system, and he was deeply critical of this.

Marx was a *historical materialist*. In other words, he believed that all societies in history could only be understood by looking at the way they organised people's labour (Marx defined labour as the natural interaction of human beings with their environment). In all societies, people's lives are defined by labour. Marx believed that labouring under capitalism defined lives in a particularly immoral way. The basis of his critique was that, under capitalism, all aspects of culture were determined by economic forces and that the overall effect of this was dehumanisation and the impoverishment of creativity. Marx believed that:

In order to buy what they need to live, people have to sell their labour power (their capacity to work) for wages. Their labour is bought and sold as a commodity: a price tag is attached to everybody. Everyone is just a means of making profit.

The exchange of labour for money is not a fair swap. Employees want to do just the amount of work required to pay for their wages. But employers need workers to create wealth far in excess of this basic requirement. So only a fraction of the working week is spent replacing the value of wages. The rest is a surplus amount of work which generates wealth for the capitalist. This is exploitation.

The goods that people produce have their natural *use value* taken away from them and replaced with false *exchange value*. Under the dominance of the market, it is not what things mean or what real purpose they serve, which counts, but how much they are worth. Everything becomes equivalent to money. Money, and not face-to-face communication, now acts as the crucial social bond.

Labour becomes for most unfulfilling and uncreative. Workers are alienated from the objects they produce and from the possibility of a truly communal life. They are prevented from fulfilling their true potential. The clash between the needs of the workers and the capitalist system results in a constant class struggle, which will eventually lead to revolution.

Society has two levels:

- the *economic base*. This is the level of the production and distribution of goods. It supports and sometimes interrupts . . .

- the *cultural superstructure*. This is the level of arts, religion, shopping, entertainment, language and party politics.

Many products of the superstructure create an insatiable consumer desire, or *commodity fetishism*. In acting as good consumers we effectively sign ourselves in to, and help to maintain, the very system which enslaves us. The superstructure tries to blind us to the true, underlying nature of capitalism. It does not let us see the economic base which creates it.

Post Marx

Baudrillard's ideas about the society of simulation are formed in part out of a dialogue with Marxism. He retained many of the touchstones of Marx's critique of modernity, but also tried to go beyond many of them. Influenced by numerous other intellectuals on the political left – and inspired by the fact that the citizens of the west seemed reluctant to unite and overthrow the system – Baudrillard believed it necessary to bring Marx up to date. Marxism had now to account for contemporary developments in information technology, consumerism, the growth of the leisure industry and multinational corporations. We are now in a period of *supermodernity, hypermodernity, late modernity, postmodernity*. Marx needs to be souped up accordingly.

In his early work, Baudrillard was in broad agreement with Marx that the expansion of capitalism had brought about fundamental social changes. He agreed that an abstract system of values had come to replace the 'real' values that (he supposed) characterised pre-modern communities, and believed that this system had penetrated much further into all aspects of existence than Marx had envisaged. Like Marx, Baudrillard claims (sometimes rather romantically) that societies before the advent of modernity possessed more 'natural' values. He believed that they enjoyed an unmediated, collective existence, uncorrupted by outside systems of value like capitalist economics. These societies were based not on productivity or the commodification of labour, but on unprofitable, supposedly spontaneous communicative activities like gift-giving, religious rituals, festivities and so on. Marx would have described such things in terms of their use value, but Baudrillard thought that in describing them that way, Marx was unwittingly projecting capitalist ideas of utility on to 'primitive' ways of life. Baudrillard preferred the phrase *symbolic exchange* to describe such pre-capitalist activities and he believed them (it is not something he could prove) to be free of the modern-day demand that everything be put to a specific purpose and given a specific value. He also differs from Marx in claiming that:

- There has been a transition from a society of production to one of reproduction. Images and information are now more important than solid commodities.

- The cultural superstructure has power of its own. It is not just a passive reflection of whatever happens in the economic base.

- Consumerism might be more important than Marx's modes and relations of production.

As a result of these factors political oppression is not located in any one specific group, place, or action. It does not come up from some underlying economic root of things. Nor is it forced down on people from above by an identifiable group of fat cat capitalists. Power is an ambience. It soaks into everything. No wonder we cannot rely on the workers to spontaneously unite in revolt.

Walter Benjamin (1892–1940)

Benjamin is relevant here because of a well-known essay he published in 1936 called *The Work of Art in the Age of Mechanical Reproduction*. In that piece, Benjamin was interested in the contribution that new technologies of mass reproduction could make to the formation of politically progressive art forms. His main contention was that with the help of these new technologies art could be removed from its high-class preserve and become available to everyone.

He noted that 'original' works of art, such as paintings, gained much of their prestige from the fact that they were usually produced in editions of one. This gave them an air of uniqueness and authority which elevated the significance of the artist's 'touch'. The work of art in all its individual glory was therefore fetishised, creating an unnecessary 'aura' around it and pushing its monetary worth to ridiculous heights.

This aura could be stripped from works of art through their multiple reproduction in colour plates, postcards, posters and so on. The new art form of cinema was also important to Benjamin for similar reasons. Baudrillard's notion of simulations as copies without originals can be traced back, at least partly, to Benjamin's argument that mass reproduction has reduced the significance of authenticity and originality.

But Baudrillard might also argue against Benjamin that, rather than destroying the aura of authenticity, the predominance of simulation replaces authenticity with *nothing but* aura. Endless reproduction of a Van Gogh painting only increases (or perhaps causes) the fame of the original and the desire to see it. If Van Gogh did not have this aura conferred upon his name by constant reproduction, who would be interested? Baudrillard would say that the endless copies only produce a nostalgic desire to confront the real thing. Yet again the real is produced by its reproduction!

Henri Lefebvre (1901–1991)

A Marxist sociologist, and at one time Baudrillard's teacher, Lefebvre is known mainly for the three volumes of his *Critique of Everyday Life* (1947–1981) in which he applied some of Marx's ideas about alienation to the conditions of day-to-day social life. Building on Marx,

Lefebvre argued that capitalism had now thoroughly colonised, or 'bureaucratised' daily existence and that people were now reduced to the status of mere consumers. Consequently, he attempted to push Marxist ideas beyond their traditional emphasis on production lines, factory floors and trade unions, and looked for signs of revolution in all aspects of life in the modern world.

Baudrillard picked up on aspects of Lefebvre's critique in his early books, *The System of Objects* (1968) and *The Consumer Society* (1970). In these, he took from Lefebvre the project of applying a Marx-informed analysis to such everyday matters as leisure pursuits, fashion, home furnishings and domestic gadgets. Influenced by Guy Debord and others (see below), he went further than Lefebvre in putting consumption rather than production on the centre stage of political theory.

Guy Debord (1931–1994)

Debord was a spokesman for a radical group of artists and social critics known as the *Situationist International*. Centred in France, and most active in the 1960s, they saw consumer and media culture as an insidious form of oppression. Believing in the power of hedonism as a force of resistance, the Situationists created art and theory which they hoped would stimulate a carnivalesque rebellion against a suffocating and falsified modern world.

In his 1967 book *The Society of the Spectacle*, Debord predicted that the economy of the later twentieth century would be driven by images rather than by the industrial production of physical goods. He argued that, with the arrival of media and consumer society, experience itself was commodified. He pointed out, for example, that we are now invited to express ourselves not through what we create, but through what we buy. Thus, to Debord, relationships were mediated by images, and social life was totally occupied by merchandise. Defining the spectacle as the 'affirmation of appearance and affirmation of all human life . . . as mere appearance', Debord argued that people could no longer take control over or actively participate in the creation of their own pleasures, experiences, and desires. People were bystanders to their own lives.

Heavily indebted to the work of Henri Lefebvre, the aim of Debord and the Situationists was therefore to turn everyday life itself into a revolutionary project – to transform the world of banality and repetition into an immediate and impassioned form of living.

Baudrillard's work is influenced in part by contacts he made with Debord in the 1960s. As you can see, his descriptions of simulation and implosion have a lot in common with Debord's account of how the spectacle and the commodity dominate social life. He also shared with Debord the feeling that the consumption of images is now more economically and politically significant than the production of objects.

However, Debord's description of the spectacle implied that he could make a clear-cut distinction between true and false. He and the Situationists also suggested that it was possible to find a certain amount of space between the spectacle and its consumers. It was in this space that liberating social change could be created. Finding that such distinctions and distances have now collapsed, Baudrillard is far less optimistic about this possibility.

Marshall McLuhan (1911–80)

McLuhan was a Canadian theorist with an interest in the impact of media on society and consciousness. His most famous book was *Understanding Media; the Extensions of Man* (1964), in which he charted the transition from print technologies to the *cool* systems of electronic media as the dominant form of communication. McLuhan argued that new technologies give birth to new human environments, and believed that over the centuries the thoughts and actions of mankind have been determined by developments in our means of communication.

For McLuhan, it was the nature of media technology (how it worked, how it had to be used, how it related to the human body), and not its content (what it showed) that was significant. He formulated this belief in the well known phrase: 'the medium is the message'.

McLuhan suggested that the media revolution of the electronic age was bringing about subtle yet momentous changes in our perceptual habits, and producing a decentralised virtual community, which he famously named the *global village*. It was thanks to *Understanding Media* that Baudrillard adopted the term *implosion* to describe the impact of this new environment. McLuhan wrote:

❝ As electrically contracted, the globe is no more than a village. Electronic speed in bringing all social and political functions together in a sudden implosion has heightened human awareness of responsibility, to an intense degree. ❞   (page 20)

As far as McLuhan was concerned, this electronic village involved a new kind of social bond and a high degree of audience participation. For instance, he cited the televised funeral of J.F. Kennedy as an occasion when the power of TV united a large mass of people in a ritual activity. Another example of this might be the images of war and famine witnessed daily on the world's TV screens. It is often claimed that the media age has enriched us with an ever expanding store of images of the world to which we would otherwise never have access, and in McLuhan's benign picture of things, this can bring people together in a rather mystical sort of technological consciousness. (Critics have pointed out that McLuhan's 'village', far from being global, is actually emitted from a very specific Euro-American centre.) Baudrillard, on the other hand, pictures the media as a much more malign force, preventing real communication or meaning and providing only a shallow, passive experience.

Baudrillard shares with McLuhan an interest in information overload, the ability of modes of communication to alter perception and the idea that the media form a sort of environment. He also borrows from McLuhan the cybernetic vision of people wired into an all-embracing image and information network. In his later 'picture book' *The Medium is the Massage* [sic] (1967) McLuhan observed:

> ❦ The wheel . . . is an extension of the foot . . . the book is an extension of the eye . . . clothing, an extension of the skin . . . electronic circuitry, an extension of the central nervous system. ❦
>
> (pages 31–40)

Later, in *Understanding Media*, he claimed that 'with TV the viewer is the screen.' (page 272).

Baudrillard echoed this vision some years later in an essay called *The Ecstasy of Communication* (in *Postmodern Culture* edited by Hal Foster, 1983):

> ❦ With the television image – the television being the ultimate and perfect object for this new era – our own body and the surrounding universe become a control screen. ❦   (page 127)

The TV screen is the retina of the mind's eye! James Woods seduced by video in David Cronenberg's *Videodrome*, 1982. BFI Stills, posters and designs.

Many of these ideas seem to have been borne out by recent developments in cybertechnology, computerisation and satellisation. Similar ideas have also appeared in works by various science fiction and cyberpunk writers of the last thirty or so years – J.G. Ballard, Phillip K. Dick, William Gibson, Bruce Sterling – and in many films – *Videodrome*, *Total Recall*, *Bladerunner*. In some of this work, we get a vision of technology out of control, taking over the human race, making its own dangerous decisions, and so on. Some writers have criticised Baudrillard for inheriting from McLuhan a similar tendency to speak of technology as if it has human motives. Baudrillard's media seem to forge themselves out of their own technological developments, as though they are independent of personal, historical, political and economic intervention.

These are just some of the thinkers whose ideas can be traced through Baudrillard's work. There are many more. Some of those other influences come from the schools of thought known as *structuralism* and *poststructuralism*. We will have a lot to say about them in the next chapter.

5

TAKING MEANING APART

In the last chapter we encountered a challenge to common sense ways of thinking about the relationship between reality and its representation. Via the work of Jean Baudrillard, we concentrated on how this challenge has arisen from a society organised around electronic media and spectacle. However, this area is only a small part of postmodern theory's concern with representation. In fact, Baudrillard's ideas are informed as much by recent theories of language and meaning as they are by theories of media and society.

So this chapter will look at a few more of the ideas about representation which have recently been seen in the light of postmodernism. Focusing on the influential body of thought known as *poststructuralism*, we will see how postmodern theory sets about dismantling most of our normal ways of thinking about how meaning works.

In order to make any sense of poststructuralism, you need to know a little about structuralism first.

Although it has had most impact in the field of literary theory and criticism, structuralism is best thought of as an approach or method rather than as a clearly defined discipline. Structuralist ideas can theoretically be used in any number of different areas – they first received widespread attention with the work of the anthropologist Claude Levi-Strauss, and also affected the thinking of the psychoanalyst Jacques Lacan – and they can be applied to many different kinds of 'text'. Also, although the term structuralism indicates a fairly restricted cluster of themes, there is not a single set of rules to which all thinkers who have been labelled structuralist will rigidly stick.

Structuralism is less concerned with what texts are about, and more with how they work. In order to see these mechanisms more clearly, structuralism deliberately plays down any notion of the content of a text (e.g. the moral of a story, the message of a folk tale). As the philosopher Jacques Derrida has noted, commenting on structuralism, 'the relief and design of structures appears more clearly when content, which is the living energy of meaning, is neutralised.' In other words, structuralism is about the formalities of *how* texts mean, rather than about *what* they mean.

At the most general level, structuralism can be seen as bringing to the fore a number of questions about meaning, representation and authorship and as exploring the relationships between language and knowledge. In this respect, it can be seen as part of a widespread pre-occupation with language which has affected a great deal of thought (including what we now call postmodernism) throughout the twentieth century. Anglo-American philosophy, in particular, has been dominated by a fascination with language, on some occasions believing that philosophy was ultimately *about* language, and that it therefore had a special ability to sort out any linguistic confusions suffered by other disciplines such as the sciences or political theory. Meanwhile, the philosopher Ludwig Wittgenstein (1889–1951) was concerned with the fact that his thought was necessarily restricted by the limits of the language in which he was bound to express them. And Martin Heidegger (1889–1976) famously claimed that 'language speaks us'.

Three main structuralist themes have influenced the development of postmodernist thought:

We use language to organise – and even construct – reality. Language enables us to give meaning to the world.

Reality cannot be readily separated from the way we represent it, or the stories we tell about it. Language therefore plays an active role in forming our perceptions of reality. This insight has been central to postmodern theory. Traces of it are clearly visible in Baudrillard's reflections on the power of simulation, for example (see previous chapter).

Meanings happen only in relation to structures.

No single thing 'gives off' a meaning of its own accord: it does so only through its relationship to other things.

Verbal and written language provides the clearest demonstration of these structural or relational properties of meaning.

Studying how language works can provide an understanding of how all cultural products create meaning.

Saussure

In the postmodern context, these ideas grew largely out of the work of Ferdinand de Saussure (1857–1913), credited as the founder of both modern linguistics and structuralism. In his *Course in General Linguistics* (first published posthumously in 1915) Saussure sought to examine the process by which language makes sense to us. He argued that in order to understand the workings of language, it was fairly pointless to look for the historical and/or 'natural' roots of particular words. Instead, words should be looked at as interrelated elements within language as a whole.

Saussure departs from previous approaches to the study of language in that he paid attention not to how it evolved over time, but to how it works as a self-governing system in the present. By denying the significance of the history of words (their etymology) and by refusing to look for their roots in nature, he anticipated the postmodern preference for surface over depth.

Words and things

Common sense tells us that the world is made up of independently existing things which naturally fit the names we have given them. This implies, for example, that there is something about a rose which means that 'rose' is inevitably the right word for it. But Saussure implies that there is no direct or causal relation between a rose and the letters R-O-S-E. Any other collection of letters could conceivably have done the job just as well. It is purely a matter of social convention that roses are called roses. Thus Saussure argued against the assumption that language is made up of individual units which have natural attachments to objects and ideas.

Because there is no natural or inevitable bond between words and things, Saussure saw language as an arbitrary system. From this starting point, structuralist – and eventually postmodernist – theory abandons any question of the 'truth' of language: it argues that language can never be a transparent or innocent reflection of reality.

A world of signs

Saussure believed that all of culture is made up of *signs*. That is to say, social life is characterised by the circulation and exchange of forms to which convention has given meaning. A sign for Saussure is simply any device through which human beings communicate to each other. To the extent that anything can have meaning attached to it, this could be taken to suggest that just about anything can be called a sign.

One implication of this is that structuralism is not, in principle, in the business of evaluating the artistic quality of its objects of enquiry. Thus there have been structuralist studies of cuisine, fashion, advertising, photography, music, movies and folk tales, among many other things. Everything is equally grist to the struturalist mill, and this generally means that it has little use for conventional discriminations between high and low culture.

A science of signs

Saussure argued that verbal and written language offered the best model of how signs made meaning through a system of arbitrary social conventions. Linguistics could therefore provide a strong basis for a scientific study of the life of signs in society. This proposed science of signs would be called *semiology* (or *semiotics*: the two are more or less interchangeable). Although structuralism and semiology are not identical in meaning, they are very closely related. It can be argued that semiology is really a branch of structuralism. It can also be claimed that semiology deals with the social and political dimension of signs, while structuralism – as its name suggests – has a more abstract concern with overall systems and underlying structures. In practice, however, there is no hard and fast distinction between the two areas.

The rules of the game

Structuralism says that language has a system of rules of combination. These rules permit a large number of different words to be created, but only within the limits of the 26 letters of alphabet. Each specific language will have its own laws regarding how letters can be strung together to make meaningful (or even pronounceable) words. We cannot do what we like with letters (or invent new ones) and expect them to make sense to anybody.

An example

Rules of *combination* in English mean that 'rose' can be rearranged to 'sore' or 'eros' and still make some sort of sense. However, English does not yet permit the letters to be recombined in any meaningful way into 'rseo'. There are also rules of *selection*. These mean that the 'o' in the same word can be substituted for a 'u' to make 'ruse', or an 'i' to make 'rise', but not for much else.

Such simple rules of course extend to how words can be put into order to create phrases, sentences, novels, poems, notes to the milkman and so on.

They also extend to all other languages. In the language of clothes, for example, the rules of selection mean that I can feasibly swap wellington boots for snow shoes, but the rules of combination decree that either kind of footwear would look rather too daring if worn in conjunction with a cocktail dress (or on the wrong part of my body).

Structuralism finds that such norms and conventions apply to all aspects of culture. Language in the sense of speech and writing simply provides the clearest embodiment of the principles which govern all sign systems.

Put at its most basic, the sign is defined by Saussure as an object, word, image, or whatever, together with its meaning. Put more technically, it is the unit of meaning produced by the relation of a *signifier* to a *signified*:

- *Signifier*: the material object, the sounds that words make, the letters on a page, etc. For example 'a bunch of red roses'.

- *Signified*: the concept or mental image to which the signifier gives rise. For example the 'romance or passion' signified by the bunch of red roses.

The signified is what is meant by the sign. The signifier is what means it.

As we saw in the case of the relationship between words and objects, the relationship between the signified and its signifier is arbitrary. For example, there is no 'natural' reason why a bunch of red roses should signify passion – it is solely a matter of convention. Culture has coded roses in this way, and we have come to take this coding for granted.

Now, the arbitrary relationship between the sign and its meaning does not suggest that you can make signs mean anything that you want them to. Individuals can neither invent signs of their own out of nothing, nor read signs in any way they please. You are never at liberty to create purely personal interpretations of things. Understanding is always in some sense constrained by rules and conventions. It is not down to personal decision that if I send red roses to someone they will most likely interpret my gesture as a romantic (or corny) one. I have not personally endowed roses with romantic connotations; they have been coded well in advance of my own amorous wishes.

So structuralism and semiology argue that the meanings of signs go far beyond individual intention. This insight is significant for the fields of art and literature, since it calls into question the modernist, romantic view of unique, original works of art being created by individual acts of genius. We will look at this question of authorship in more detail later.

Signs of difference

The established difference between 'rose' and 'nose' is what allows a different meaning to be given to each of those otherwise identical words. In the English language the sound 'r' and the sound 'n' are registered as distinct enough to be granted significance. It is conceivable that another language would not recognise the distinction between the two sounds (or would not make it significant). Neither 'r' nor 'n' have much to say by themselves. They get meaning only by virtue of what other letters they are combined with.

Roses signify passion and romance partly because they are not poppies or chrysanthemums.

It is also important that roses are on the correct side of the arbitrary distinction we make between flowers and weeds. Few people would receive a bunch of weeds as a sign of affection.

These are all illustrations of the structuralist principle that signs mean what they do because of what the structure of language allows. In this view, signs have significance (that is, they are indeed signs) only in relation to language as a whole. Thus Saussure places little weight on isolated signs. His only concern is for relationships between signs within a self-sufficient system of differences. The meaning of a sign is never its own, special, private property but is the product of its difference from other signs.

Structuralists at work

The suggestions touched on above have been picked up in many different ways. Here are a few examples.

The System of Objects (1968) Jean Baudrillard

Interior decoration and domestic furniture can be analysed as sign systems structured like language. Modernity brings about a new commodification and regulation of everyday life, in which it becomes important to keep up with fashion, and to assemble goods (e.g. clothes, household furnishings) in such a way that they:

- go together and
- differentiate you (your taste, social class, etc.) from others.

Under capitalism all rooms in the middle-class home are structured around systems of goods (e.g. the 'country kitchen' look). The domestic environment is a system of objects and styles, designed to function under the logic of modernity: life gets taken over by a consumer ambience in which all commodities get their meaning from their position in networks of commodity-signs.

A particular style of armchair signifies not by itself, but in relation: to understand it, you should look at its relation to the suite of which it is a part, the suite's relation to the decor of the room, its relation to other available designs, the relationship between the theme of the lounge and the theme of other rooms in the house, and the way your possessions are encoded with mass-produced signs of 'individuality'.

Signs and Meaning in the Cinema (1972) Peter Wollen

The structuralist film critic should be on the look-out for a system of
differences and oppositions. In looking at the films of a single director,
the structuralist film critic is not concerned with the obvious repetition
of storylines and styles through a number of films produced over that
director's career. Rather, he or she is looking for an underlying *esoteric
structure* of binary oppositions that reveals a *whole complex of meaning* beneath the entire spectrum of the film maker's work. Studying
the Westerns of John Ford would reveal changing expressions of the
binary oppositions 'garden vs. desert', 'civilisation vs. savagery' and
'heroes vs. villains'. These oppositions are social constructs with political implications. Moveover, they are not produced solely out of the
head of the individual director: individuals are seen by structuralism
as mere channels or transmitters of social meanings. In self-expression
we repeat ideals unconsciously, without being aware of their wider
resonances.

Decoding Advertisements (1978) Judith Williamson

Williamson saw advertising as a subtle form of propaganda designed
only to buy us into capitalism. Structuralism and semiotics are the
tools which enable us to take advertising apart and reveal its true
mechanisms. Adverts produce meanings which have no direct connection to reality. They are all about trying to establish differences
between items that Williamson argues are essentially the same.
Aftershave adverts create very particular images for specific products
so that they appear radically different from other bottles of (very similar) fragrant liquid. Two brands of instant coffee do not differ from
one another, but advertising campaigns work to differentiate them in
order to stimulate false desires, and they do this through their own
internal organisation of words and images. Adverts are specific structures of signs which work by making connections between things. An
obvious example is that of a cigarette advert: the coming together of
the brand name and the image of a cowboy on horseback creates a
chain of association between smoking, masculity, health, activity and
the great outdoors.

On one level, the advert itself is the signifier (the material sign), while
the product is the signified (the concept referred to). On another level,
the product becomes a signifier, while its signifieds are the connotations given by the structure of the advert as a whole. This structure

allows the meaning of one sign (e.g. the cowboy) to be transferred to another (e.g. the brand name).

A postmodern criticism of Williamson

In his book *Postmodernism; The Twilight of the Real* (1990) Neville Wakefield criticises Williamson's structuralist approach. He sees it as relying on outmoded modernist principles of depth analysis. Williamson sees ads only in terms of their deep meaning – to persuade us to buy the product. A postmodern view would emphasise the pleasures we might gain from the advert itself without taking much of an interest in the commodity it refers to. Postmodern ways of 'reading' media involve zapping between channels, flicking through magazines, surfing the Internet, cruising the multiplex and so on.

None of these are particularly suggestive of deep meanings or persuasion by secret forces. The postmodern consumer is a nomadic sort of window-shopper, capable of sampling a multitude of experiences thrown up by culture, but without having to have any special personal attachment to them.

The rationalist notion of deep meaning implied by structuralism and other modern forms of analysis is therefore made inappropriate by postmodernism. Dick Hebdige makes a similar point (though he is rather less enthusiastic about it) in his 1988 book, *Hiding in the Light*:

❝ Cruising was originally introduced as a poststructuralist strategy for going beyond the puritanical confinement of critical activity to the pursuit and taming . . . of the ideological signified. By cruising the 'reader' can take pleasure in a text without being obliged at the same time to take marriage vows and a mortgage on a house. ❞

(page 162)

Poststructuralism

We have seen that structuralism asks where meaning comes from. Does it come from the text itself? Does it come from the context in which the text is consumed? Is the reader free to create his or her own meaning? To what degree can the author of a text control how it is interpreted? Does the production of meaning arise from the interaction of these factors? If so, exactly how do they interact?

Poststructuralism continues to ask these questions.

We have noted elsewhere that structuralism and poststructuralism form much of the philosophical background of postmodern theory. Indeed, nowadays poststructuralism is often seen as postmodern philosophy. One of the dangers of this is that it can give the impression that poststructuralism is a single school of thought or academic discipline. In fact, the term is regularly used to unite the work of a fairly diverse group of thinkers, few of whom ever described themselves as poststructuralists. Also, although the word 'poststructuralism' implies that it simply took over from structuralism at some point in history, it is truer to say that, especially in the 1960s and 1970s, the two ran alongside each other and often crossed tracks.

Nevertheless it is safe to note certain major currents in poststructuralist thought. What the various poststructuralists have in common are:

- the questions listed
- the fact that their work mixes together political theory, literary criticism, philosophy, psychoanalytical theory, semiotics, structuralism and (in some cases) feminism
- the great density of many of their writings.

They inherit from structuralism the following three broad (and overlapping) ideas:

- language cannot point outside of itself
- languages produce (rather than reflect) meaning
- language does not express individuality.

So there are certain similarities between poststructuralism and its supposed predecessor. But it has the prefix 'post-' partly because it takes the implications of structuralism further than the likes of Saussure and Levi-Strauss probably intended. There is also the important fact that it parts company with structuralism on a number of (again overlapping) points. For convenience, we can divide these into three as well:

Poststructuralism is more anti-foundational

Structuralism removed texts from the foundations of reality and individual authorship. In this way we may call it an anti-foundational tendency. But it also suggested that although texts can be seen as flat surfaces, they are supported by deep, hidden, fundamental structures. However, poststructuralism can be seen as rejecting any such notion of ultimate, underlying grounds beneath meaning.

Poststructuralism is less all-embracing

Poststructuralists accuse structuralism of too often setting itself up arrogantly as a superior, objective viewpoint from which to observe eternal 'global facts' behind all texts. Poststructuralists see this as a totalitarian or imperialist attitude which suppresses the significance of specific minds working in particular social and historical contexts. Poststructuralists do not believe that it is possible or desirable to step outside of your objects of study and unveil a final, all-embracing explanation of everything.

Poststructuralism makes more of difference

Structuralism claimed that in language no sign had a positive meaning on its own terms. Meaning was always a product of difference. Despite this, language was seen as a relatively fixed and stable, even tyrannical, structure.

Poststructuralism brings difference into the foreground, in order to disrupt any notion of stability or unity of meaning.

In structuralism, a text is often seen as complete. In poststructuralism, it is always unfinished, full of holes, and contradictory.

—— Poststructuralists at work ——

Pierre Macherey

Macherey was a Marxist critic working within the structuralist/poststructuralist arena. As a Marxist, he was concerned with how texts act to reproduce the values of capitalism. He followed the tradition within Marxist-orientated literary theory of believing that the way we habitually consume texts (and other commodities) is more or less passive and unquestioning.

So as to survive, the status quo has to give the impression of being in good working order. It also has to persuade people that the current state of affairs is simply the way things are. In other words, it has to distract people from the idea that their conditions of existence are the direct result of a historically specific social and economic structure. For Macherey, most texts and their consumers participate in creating and maintaining the taken-for-granted illusion that the status quo is inevitable, coherent and unchangeable. In short, texts (and the way we have learned to consume them) aim to reconcile us to our conditions.

They do this by creating a certain sense of smoothness, or unity. For example, when we watch most films, we tend to be interested only in the events they describe. The questions we ask concern only what is going to happen next and whether a particular character is going to win the day. Thus, whenever we admire or identify with a film star, or simply follow the actions of a character on screen, we very rarely think about acting as a form of work, or film as a form of industrial production. We give little thought to studio trade union disputes going on behind the scenes, or to the unequal pay structures between technical staff and actors. We are effectively blind to these aspects of film production, and Macherey would argue that we create this blindness for ourselves by letting ourselves be sucked into the film's unfolding yarn.

We ignore the complex pattern of edits, flashbacks, jump-cuts and all the other devices that go into the fabrication of a movie. In fact, most films are really very fragmented, highly complicated pieces of material, but in the process of viewing this fact gets lost. By getting involved (or trying to get involved) in the stories they tell, we unconsciously stitch a multitude of filmic elements (for example, frames, scenes, shots and sequences) together into an intelligible sequence. In this way attention is drawn away from the social, economic and political context in which the film is made.

For Macherey, all texts only just succeed in achieving such a sense of smoothness. Chaos is always bubbling away just under the surface. The text could easily fall into turmoil, if only we would let it. For texts are really constructed out of ill matching bits and pieces, holes, contradictions, and dislocations.

Summary

In contrast to the structuralist project of looking for the fundamental order behind texts, Macherey searches for chaos beneath the illusion of coherence: 'the concealed order of the work is . . . less significant than its real *determinate* disorder (its disarray)'. Always on the look-out for the barely hidden moments of repression and division in texts which attempt to present a coherent world view, Macherey argues that all texts are really assembled from a diverse rag-bag of different ideas. These ideas may be in conflict with each other, and may be found to disrupt or challenge a given text's intended overt message.

Texts not only try to cover over their own internal gaps and conflicts, but are created out of the meanings they omit or repress: what a text puts 'outside' of itself determines what it says.

Key work: *Theory of Literary Production* (1966) (first English translation 1978)

In other words

Whereas structuralism saw language as a closed system, and tried to fix individual texts to rigid linguistic frameworks, poststructuralism tries to open texts up and cut meanings loose. Poststructuralists do not necessarily believe that everything is meaningless, just that meaning is never *final*.

Julia Kristeva

Although very difficult to summarise adequately, Julia Kristeva's large and complex body of work can be seen partly as a feminist expression of poststructuralist theory. That is to say, she brings gender politics into the poststructuralist frame. Having said that, it is worth remembering that she is not particularly interested in such feminist projects as rediscovering great works of literature written by women, or in looking at the stereotypes by which women are misrepresented. Drawing on psychoanalytical theory as well as structuralism and semiotics, she is concerned with more abstract connections between language or literature and gender.

Kristeva believes that it is possible to create a 'feminine' voice in literature. But she also denies the idea that there is some essential, timeless category of womanliness from which this voice can come. For Kristeva, no text can express a universal, authentic feminine experience which is then re-experienced by the reader.

Women may not be *born* with an ability to speak in a 'feminine' tongue. But they are pushed to the edges – or put outside of – 'mainstream' systems of representation. As an example of this, note that I (being male) have just referred to women as 'they', and that it is still common for writers to use 'he' and 'mankind' to refer to people in general. In this way women can be said to be linguistically silenced. Kristeva goes on to argue that they can use this marginal position as a space from which to create subversion. Thus it is possible to produce writing (and also ways of reading) which goes beyond what Kristeva sees as conventionally masculine values like rigour, intelligibility, stability, and structure. She argues that texts (and literary critics) should produce playful, diverse, slippery and unstable meanings; these can effect a pleasurable and progressive undermining of masculine language.

The self on trial

Kristeva argues that male-dominated society discourages multiple forms of selfhood (see Chapters 6 and 7 for a detailed consideration of this). Partly because our language only allows for she/he, her/him and so on, our identities are largely confined to rigid gender definitions. However, certain experimental ways of using language can, for Kristeva, anarchically shake up the traditional definitions of self.

In her book *Revolution in Poetic Language*, Kristeva claimed that the language of avant-garde poetry and literature could help to loosen identity and free it from socially imposed limitations. 'Marginal texts' could be produced which disturbed the imaginary positions of identification that readers normally take on in the act of reading. 'Difficult' or 'transgressive' texts (for example Joyce's *Finnegans Wake*, the plays of Antonin Artaud) prevent the illusion of being passively swept along with unfolding fictional events. For Kristeva, as for some other of her poststructuralist colleagues, such acts of identification are the products of habit and serve only to confirm the way you already see yourself. Marginal works, on the other hand, contribute to what Kristeva sees as a revolutionary, liberating undoing of the imagined unity of the self.

Summary

Progressive works of art for Kristeva are fragmentary, incomplete, non-systematic, and ultimately inexplicable. They subvert normal, mainstream language, and in doing so put gendered identities on trial. In other words experimental uses of language can free people from the limits of gender.

A note of caution

One criticism of this is that Kristeva's ideas, like those of Macherey, seem mainly to be defences of non-mainstream literature. They have little respect for popular or mass culture. It could be argued that their theories are in this way elitist. To put it bluntly, can the kind of literature promoted by Kristeva really be as 'progressive' as she thinks it can if hardly anybody bothers to read it? Is hers a theory of what she thinks everybody else should be reading? And if so, what gives her the right to do this?

Key works: *Revolution in Poetic Language* (1974) (English translation 1984)
Desire in Language: A Semiotic Approach to Literature and Art (1980)

Jacques Derrida

We often wonder what people are really getting at by certain comments they make. We wonder what celebrities are really like. When we read a novel or poem, we wonder what its message is. When a shocking crime takes place, we wonder whether its true cause lies in the inherent evil of the criminal, something awful in his or her upbringing, or the fact that he or she was an avid viewer of violent films. In these and a thousand other ways we are used to talking about things as though they have an essential meaning or root cause.

As you know, postmodern thought tends to reject the idea of things having a single, basic meaning. Instead, it embraces fragmentation, conflict and discontinuity in matters of history, identity and culture. It is suspicious of any attempt to provide all-embracing, total theories. And it rejects the view that any cultural phenomenon can be explained as the effect of one objectively existing, fundamental cause.

One of the most influential figures in this postmodern turn of thought against originals, centres and foundations is Jacques Derrida (born 1930). In a long series of extremely demanding books published since the mid 1960s, Derrida has developed his own particular poststructuralist blend of philosophy, linguistics, and literary analysis. It goes by the name of *deconstruction*.

Derrida's deconstructive work is very much a part of the project, discussed throughout this chapter, of questioning what we might call the meaning of meaning. It continues the structuralist task of looking for the conditions which allow texts to be meaningful, and it shares their interest in the relationships between language and thought. However, in common with the poststructuralist topics we have discussed so far, Derrida is much more interested in how the meanings of texts can be plural and unstable than in fixing them to a rigid structure.

Conditions of knowledge

If your doctor started to rhapsodise over the aesthetic properties of a rash on your neck instead of offering a proper diagnosis of it, you would probably feel that they were finding the wrong kind of 'meaning' there. But this is not to say that their 'reading' of your rash is simply false, or that it is a misinterpretation of the facts. Rather than being inaccurate, it is simply out of place. Criteria from the field of art are being transported into the field of medicine. In other words, your doctor is going too far outside the confines of medical discourse. Meanings always have a place.

This is an example of how, as Derrida argues, fields of knowledge always put a necessary limit on what can and cannot be validly said. Any discourse – medical, artistic, legal, or whatever – is defined by the methods and understandings it makes available to its practitioners, and as such prevents meanings from ever spinning off in inappropriate directions.

According to Derrida, particular disciplines present meanings and truths as obvious. In fact, though, what counts as meaning or truth is determined by the limitations of the discipline which supposedly 'discovers' and describes them. One of Derrida's projects is to show that all meanings and truths are never absolute or timeless, but are always framed by socially and historically specific conditions of knowledge. So when your doctor finally gets round to offering a diagnosis of your rash, they are actually bringing into play a great deal of particular ideas about what counts as an illness, how symptoms relate to diseases and what doctors are for.

None of these things are outside of history and culture. Likewise, what they prescribe as a cure will depend on current conditions of knowledge, and these may well be subject to change (a cure today can turn out to be a poison tomorrow).

Of course, none of these issues enters into your conversation with your doctor. You will just want to get your prescription and go home. Consulting your GP for medical advice simply seems like a perfectly normal thing to do, and neither you nor your doctor is therefore likely to discuss the field of medicine as a social construct. The field of medicine, we might say, involves certain historically particular notions of illness, symptom, and cure. It also depends on certain western ideas about scientific rationality and objectivity. For example, modern western medicine presents itself as a science and thus as fundamentally opposed to magic. All fields of knowledge structure themselves around touchstones of their own making in this way, yet fail to draw attention to their process of construction.

To take a slightly different example, literary theorists and critics tend to present their activity of interpreting texts as though it were an obvious or natural thing to do. They do not tell us why literary criticism might be a worthwhile way of making a living, or on what grounds some texts but not others are said to count as literature. Both literature and criticism are therefore taken for granted, as if they were self-evident facts of life. Thus it is possible for a critic to make use of an inherited set of critical criteria without ever having to reveal or question it. Most film reviewers are a case in point: they never question the validity of seeing directors as the main authors who give meanings to films. Meaning is regarded as a 'presence' in the text, and the critic believes he or she somehow has a special power to drag it into the light.

--------------------- # Conclusion ---------------------

Deconstruction discovers hidden assumptions. There is no 'pure' knowledge outside of society, culture, or language.

Against presence

Thinking of things in terms of what they 'really mean' is a habit of thought which seems perfectly natural to us, and it is hard to imagine an alternative to it. For example, I am writing here about a group of texts as if they form a single body of work which belongs to a single author (Derrida) and in which we find certain basic themes. I have also mentioned postmodern thought as if it represented a single slab of knowledge. If there *is* a single main aim in Derrida's work, it is nothing less ambitious than to dismantle this habit of thought, which he sees as an illusory belief in certainty and *presence*.

By presence, Derrida means that western forms of knowledge – in science, philosophy, 'common sense', and so on – build themselves up on certain 'centres' and 'origins'. One of the main concerns of deconstruction is to show that those centres and origins have no basis in reality. They are myths. (This should alert you to the fact that it is dangerous to speak of Derrida having a single project, or of deconstruction having a main concern.)

Derrida's criticism of presence both develops and argues with Saussure's structuralism. He takes from Saussure the idea that language cannot point outside of itself. In other words, language is a self-referring, self-regulating system. For structuralism, you do not need to look outside of a sign-system in order to find meaning: meaning is produced by the internal relationships between parts. Thus structuralism refused to find the source of meaning in nature or in the author.

Derrida and poststructuralism agree with structuralism on this point. They both reject the significance of personal intentions or individual experience in the creation of meaning. What counts for both is not intentional self-expression but the operation of the languages we inherit: the means of representation both exceed and precede decisions made by individual human beings.

But Derrida argues that structuralism chickens out of expanding on this theme. He claims that although structuralism rejects individuality and nature as pure grounds of meaning. It still holds on to a *depth model* of meaning. In other words, it assumes that you can use structuralist ideas to cut through the surface of a text and get at its true linguistic machinery. It can 'solve' texts.

So structuralism changed where meanings were thought to come from, but it still gave meaning a source in the rigorous structure of language itself. For example, Claude Levi-Strauss thought he had found a single universal structure beneath all (only superficially diverse) cultures.

Derrida calls this the *metaphysics of presence*, and it involves the myth that things are meaningful before we give words to them.

For example, because we have the single word 'postmodernism', we assume that there is also a single thing in existence to which the word corresponds. The *name* 'postmodernism' has thus in effect given rise to the *thing* so that we can now find ourselves asking 'what is postmodernism?' rather than the more appropriate question 'what does the word postmodernism do?' Derrida would say that we have succumbed once again to the metaphysics of presence: postmodernism has become an object (a presence) in such a way that we can speak of some things as being more postmodern than others.

It is by reference to such presences that interpretations and theories can claim to represent valid pieces of information. But Derrida's deconstruction seeks to expose how the language used in particular fields both creates the essential presence through which knowledge can claim to be true, and conceals the means by which it creates this presence.

——— Deconstructing opposites ———

As we hinted at in the case of our doctor's hidden assumptions about the clear distinction between science and magic, the sense of presence constructed by fields of knowledge relies heavily on systems of opposition. In this medical example, 'science' is the preferred or dominant term (the presence), while 'magic' is the inferior term against which the scientific can be defined. By putting itself on the 'correct' side of the opposition, science constructs itself as the site of objectivity and truth.

Derrida argues that all thought performs such arbitrary acts of splitting. Thus we habitually think with such oppositions as good/evil, inside/outside, private/public, nature/culture, body/soul, positive/negative, objective/subjective. One half of the distinction is always seen as inferior to, derivative of, less than, disruptive of or expressive of the other half, which in this process gets privileged as the pure, primary presence. There is always a bias towards one term over the other, and this becomes the assumed grounds for argument, interpretation and proof.

Arguments about the nature of postmodernism often act in a similar way. Whether for or against postmodernism, they often set it up (as the word itself suggests) in terms of its relation (of opposition/continuity, etc.) to a notion of modernism. In this way, modernism becomes a single thing, created in retrospect by its supposed 'post'. In this process both modernism and postmodernism come to define each other. Arguments about what postmodernism is, or what its effects are, can then proceed on the basis that it differs in some way from something that it has itself helped to make.

Inside out/outside in

In order to make this book make as much sense as possible, I have had to hold back a great many difficulties and contradictions. I have had to make all sorts of decisions about what to include and what to exclude. I have had to draw relatively firm lines around different points in history, and between different theoretical points of view. On the other hand, I have had to suggest continuities, influences and ongoing trends, where you could just as easily find fracture, conflict and diversity. Finally, I have constantly had to decide how far back to go in tracing the history of an idea, and how far away from the supposed crux of the issue I should go in explaining various strands and influences.

So this book gets its identity from the mass of things I have decided *not* to write about. If I put some of these rejected aspects back into the text (if I made different choices about what is and what is not crucial) you would have a different book in your hands.

All of these are part of how you try to build a reasonably coherent text, especially one with the aim of being 'introductory'. But *all* texts, and not just introductory ones, work in the same way to create an *illusion of coherence*. The task of deconstruction is to show that this is a very precarious illusion. It would show that what this book allows you to see as *central* is created by what I have decided is *marginal*. This book *is* therefore partly what it *is not*.

When Derrida deconstructs a text, he goes for details which give away this process. He brings back into the foreground the very things which the text pretends it does not need. He looks for what he calls the *present absences*, or *productive silences*. Sometimes he analyses the footnotes of books in more detail than the main thrust of the argument. Footnotes are bits of added information, little pieces of disagreement or possible contradiction which the author leaves outside. To let them back in again would upset the main body of the text, would mess up the argument, and so this is precisely what Derrida's deconstruction does.

Summary

Although deconstruction sets itself the task of digging up the hidden suppressions and exclusions upon which texts are constructed, it is far from being an act of interpretation in the normal sense. Deconstruction does not mean trying to root out what a text is 'really saying'. On the contrary, it tries to show that the grounds from which texts and theories seem to proceed are always shifting and unstable. One way it achieves this is by recognising the active role played by the invisible or marginalised in any text. Another is by exposing a text's system of imaginary oppositions.

Conclusion

- Western philosophies (including everyday common sense) revolve around an illusory *metaphysics of presence*. This can be found in myths about 'essence', 'meaning', 'cause', and 'self'.

- But such presence is never purely *present*. Essential meanings are not *just there*: they are *put there* by the tools, knowledges and assumptions we use to look for them.

- What counts as the deep or central meaning of a text depends on where you stand.

- The language we use to put names to things plays an important part in identifying those things for us in the first place.

- All theories, arguments, texts, etc. rest on abstract systems of relationships. So they never touch down on the sure grounds of a preexisting and pure reality.

- Structuralism sought the 'facts' about texts. For poststructuralism (and so for postmodernism) there are no facts. There are only interpretations.

Writing

When trying to get to grips with poststructuralism we might well ask 'what is Derrida talking about?' In literature classes, teachers often ask their students what a particular piece of writing is 'saying'. In both of these cases, we are confusing writing with speech. But for Derrida and poststructuralism, there is no author speaking to us: there is only writing on a page.

Derrida argues (or rather, I infer from writing with the name 'Derrida' attached to it) that all sciences and philosophies deny writing any significance. Writing is presented as a merely convenient medium of communication through which ideas can be transmitted. First, there is the idea. Second, this gets written down. Third, the idea is communicated by the writing to the reader. In other words, we are under the impression that writing is transparent: we can look through it and see the thoughts on the other side.

Philosophical, scientific, and other forms of factual writing therefore traditionally prosper under the illusion that writing is neutral. In a scientific paper, or in a news item, you are not invited to pay attention to the language being used. To look at the writing itself (e.g. the words, the style) would seem beside the point: you should be looking beyond them to the argument or to the facts.

But Derrida's work, and that of the other poststructuralists, rejects the idea that writing can simply be a window to the truth. Rather, it prefers to see writing as opaque. Take a piece of writing from any newspaper, for example. It presents itself – or we are used to reading it as though it presents itself – as an innocent bit of reportage. We are of course aware that sometimes newspapers get their facts wrong, and we know that they are often selective in what they tell us, but structuralism and poststructuralism would go further than that: they would look, not at how the article told (or failed to tell) the truth, but at the way language itself was being used. The idea that language is transparent serves only to distract attention from the possibility that the story could have been told in any number of other ways. The use of different words can, for instance, create very different meanings (classic examples include the choice of 'mob' over 'crowd' and 'terrorist' over 'freedom fighter'). The idea that language is neutral denies that writing always sets up particular constructions of reality, and that these constructions are always tied in to history, society and politics. For deconstructionists, there is no such thing as neutral language.

It is on similar grounds that people often argue over political correctness in matters of language and representation. Like advertisers, governments are also aware of the power of words to affect thoughts. The British government, for example, has recently made its Department of Social Security call unemployed people 'Jobseekers' and changed their Income Support into 'Jobseeker's Allowance'.

So poststructuralists insist that all texts are opaque writing more than approximate versions of direct speech. We (mistakenly) tend to believe that when someone speaks, the words which come out of their mouths are like hot-lines to the thoughts in their head, and can therefore be trusted. Writing, by contrast, does not, for the poststructuralist, have this privilege (and neither does speech, really, for speech too is a form of writing). So suggesting that all texts are opaque means suggesting that no texts can be trusted. We should always beware the ruses used by texts to convince us of their innocence and honesty.

These sorts of ideas have been used by many critics to praise texts which deliberately draw attention to their style or to the way they are put together. It is claimed that in doing this, certain texts reject any pretence of being neutral.

An example of this is the film *Schindler's List*. Steven Spielberg's film about the Holocaust is in grainy black and white, with some sequences in colour. This reminds us of the constructed or artificial nature of the film, the fact that we are watching a length of celluloid rather than reality unfolding. This acknowledges that no single film can adequately express the enormity of the real historical events. It acknowledges that it is a partial version of those events, constructed by Spielberg and his team in the limited form of a three-hour mainstream movie.

By highlighting its own artificiality (the clearest example being a monochrome sequence in which one girl's raincoat is coloured red), the film can be said to admit that it cannot, on its own, tell the whole story. It is, after all, only a film.

In addition to this, you might find similar distancing strategies in many other recent examples. To take just three: there has been a rise in fairly unintelligible typography on record covers, club flyers and so on. The opening titles of the 1995 film *Seven* are similarly deliberately scratchy and rough looking (the *Seven* look has recently been imitated in many TV commercials). Many pop videos combine different looks and textures by mixing Hi-8 video sequences with 16mm celluloid, letterbox formats with full-screen, monochrome with colour. You can probably think of many more examples like this. All of these can perhaps be called *deconstructive practices* in that they, like visual speech marks, draw attention to their own physical materials.

Some of these ideas have influenced the work of a number of theorists concerned with the cultural politics of representation. For example, Trinh T. Minh-Ha has written some interesting pieces on the subjective (and never 'neutral') techniques of documentary film-making (see her book *When the Moon Waxes Red* (1991) for more on this).

—————— **Concluding thoughts** ——————

We come across many examples of the postmodern *anti-foundational* attitude in this book. In this chapter we have seen Jacques Derrida and Pierre Macherey criticise the structuralists for their faith in a basic order beneath the surface of texts. In the last chapter we looked at Jean Baudrillard's argument that, in a society of simulation, images float free of reality and find a reality of their own. And in the following two chapters, we will see the impact that similar ideas have had on our ideas about the self. In all of these ways and many more postmodernism has abandoned the idea that anything is simply founded on a single, objectively existing, stable ground.

Two very influential schools of thought in particular – Marxism and Freudian psychoanalysis – have been modified and criticised at the hands of this postmodern suspicion of foundations. The traditional Marxist claim that everything which happens in culture is, at the end of the day, a reflection of fundamental conditions within the capitalist economic base has been brought to book by some brands of postmodern theory. And as we will see in the following chapter, the Freudian belief that the mental states of adults have their universal origins in infancy and in unconscious drives has similarly been criticised for being too *foundational*.

Doubts

Because this gives rise to the idea that there are no firm truths, but only versions of the truth, critics of Derrida find in his work a kind of nihilism. They see it as an 'anything goes', 'nothing is real' philosophy in which everything is equally meaningless. So it is no longer possible to have an opinion on anything, political and moral values are neutralised, there is no point trying to understand anything, we might as well give up and submit to anarchy.

Defence

Derrida's ideas can be seen as having a more progressive potential in the sense that:

- they ask us to look for the assumptions embedded in widespread beliefs and dogmas
- they suggest we should always question the grounds on which we feel able to make value judgements
- they make us aware that we always think and act from a particular position
- there is no objective point of view which gives access to a pure global truth
- thus we can (and must) always remain open to new possibilities.

We will have more to say about these ideas in Chapter 8.

Two key works by Derrida:

Of Grammatology (1967) (English translation 1976)
Writing and Difference (1967) (English translation 1978)

6

IDENTITY CRISIS

As the title suggests, this chapter will look at how ideas about personal identity have been affected by postmodernism. We will look at how the escalation of modernity's technological and social transformations have been claimed to bring conventional ideas about personal identity into serious doubt. And we will look at a few of the recent theoretical positions – drawn from several different academic fields – which have sought to provide new postmodern accounts of what it means to have or to 'be' an identity. As we will see, these accounts have had enormous implications. To take just two rather large examples: they have had important repercussions in thinking about issues of gender and sexuality. And they have concerned the relationships between identity and location (for example national identity).

There are many sides to the unfolding story of postmodern identity, but if there is one central theme, it is that *the self is fundamentally social*. Of course postmodernism did not invent this basic observation. It has been around for a long time. Karl Marx, for one, insisted on it, and sociology is in some respects founded on the idea. Nevertheless, postmodernism does inflect the notion of the social self in its own particular ways. For Jean Baudrillard (see Chapter 4) it involves a viral invasion of simulation into private life, such that it is impossible to draw a line between natural and manufactured identities and desires. For critics like Douglas Kellner and Angela McRobbie it has meant a consideration of how senses of identity can be constructed by the consumption of mass-produced objects and images. For others, as we will see in the following chapter, the outcome has been a re-think of the idea of self-expression in art and other forms of production.

Many different models of a 'postmodern self' have been built up on the idea of the social self. But a certain cluster of different questions keep recurring:

- What are the limits of the self?

- What is the relationship between private and public or inner and outer selves? Is it possible to differentiate them in any clear way?

- Is the self whole, unified, singular? Or is it more appropriate to speak of plural or fragmented selves?

— The changing nature of the self —

In his essay 'Popular Culture and the Construction of Postmodern Identities' (in *Modernity and Identity*, edited by Lash and Friedman, 1992) Douglas Kellner describes what he sees as the transition to postmodern modes of identity. His description basically maps three stages:

1 Pre-modern identity

In pre-modern communities identity is social, but it is not beset by doubt or conflict. Personal identity is stable, because it is defined and maintained by long-standing myths and pre-defined systems of roles. You are part of an age-old kinship system. Your thought and behaviour are enclosed within a limited world view, and the direction your life is going to take is more or less determined for you. Thus there is no need to question your place in the world. Identity is not an issue.

You might note that Kellner suggests this view of the pre-modern past is a piece of anthropological folklore based on wishful thinking more than on fact. You can also find traces of wishful thinking in Jean Baudrillard's notion of 'traditional' cultures based on symbolic exchange (see Chapter 4), as well as in the work of a number of other thinkers who have tried to define the specific character of contemporary identity. However, Kellner does not offer an alternative view of pre-modern societies to replace this rather mythical one.

2 Modern identity

In the modern period (starting with the Enlightenment), identity entered into crisis for the first time. As in pre-modern cultures, your personal identity remains based on your relations with others. It retains a degree of stability, but its orientations and influences start to multiply. Where in pre-modern communities you knew exactly what your place was in the clan, modern societies begin to offer a wider range of social roles. As Kellner puts it, 'One is a mother, a son, a Texan, a Scot, a professor, a sociologist, a Catholic, a lesbian – or rather a combination of these social roles and possibilities'.

There are therefore expanded possibilities for what you can be. It becomes possible to start choosing your identity, rather than simply being born into it. You start to worry about who you really are and what you should be doing with your life. With this new self-consciousness about who you are, could be or should be, you become more desperate to achieve a recognised, stable identity. You begin to worry that your identity may be transient, fragile or false. This is all part of the peculiarly modern form of identity.

There is still assumed to be a real, innate self underneath the public roles you play, but the struggle is in finding it and being true to it. Hand in hand with these widespread concerns, philosophers also begin to question the nature of the self, and as time goes on the questions become more anxious. Sigmund Freud and psychoanalysis go in search of the roots of the self and find them caught between unconscious instincts and the bourgeois family. At the same time, the discipline of sociology is developed and insists that all identities have their basis in society and that they have to be studied not as some abstract entity, but in terms of how they interact with other social beings in specific social situations. Modern sociologists argue, in general, that primary encounters such as those in the home and at school help to form a relatively permanent core identity which underlies your social activities throughout adult life.

Modernity involves the belief that rejecting the shackles of tradition will forward the progress towards human emancipation. But promoting the present and the future and negating the past as a foundation for action and selfhood forces people to question the nature of their identity.

In short, identity becomes an 'issue'.

3 Postmodern identity

Social life is faster and more complex than it was in modernity. More and more demands are placed on us, more and more possible identities are paraded before us, we have to juggle a rapidly expanding number of roles as society starts to fragment.

Some theorists (for example Jameson, Baudrillard, Debord – see Chapter 4) start to look at how the selves achieved under modernity have vanished in the wake of consumerism, mass culture, and growing bureaucratisation of life. Others, (such as Lacan and Foucault – see below) propose that the stable, unified self has always been an illusion. Although identity remains an issue in day-to-day life, postmodern theorists have binned any notion of the self as substantial, essential or timeless. In place of the serious modernist search for the deep, authentic self, we have a recognition, and sometimes a celebration, of disintegration, fragmented desires, superficiality, and identity as something you shop for. According to some sociologists identity is best understood in terms of role play or style management (see the section on Erving Goffman below). Image is now all that matters. In some earlier twentieth-century philosophy, the self loses its substance and becomes the product of your own search for authenticity (for example the work of Jean-Paul Sartre). In postmodernism the self is still without substance, but fashion statements, shopping and lifestyle choices have pushed authenticity out of the equation.

This is an admittedly simplistic history of changing ideas about personal identity, but it does serve to bring some important themes to light. We will now examine these themes in more detail by looking at some of the landmarks in the terrain of postmodern identities.

——— The stylisation of life ———

Commentators like Kellner approach the postmodern self by arguing that certain social conditions have produced in people a heightened awareness of appearance and style. In following this line of enquiry they trace how the making of identity has become increasingly related to what we buy (or want to buy). We now forge our identities by using goods as signals of both individuality (difference from social groups) and solidarity (a sense of belonging to other social groups). In this process identity has been freed from its 'pre-modern' foundations. Yet, as David Harris explains in his book, *A Society of Signs* (1996):

> ❝ As the consumer market is flexible and more dynamic than the older ways of regulating identities, much more fluidity is apparent: people can change their identities more frequently, experiment with them, select more options from a cultural supermarket with far less commitment than before. ❞   (page 207)

This is lifestyle shopping, and it involves what some critics have termed the *aestheticisation* or *stylisation* of life. In his book *Consumer Culture and Postmodernism* (1991) Mike Featherstone relates this stylised self to the emergence of a number of postmodern social and cultural developments which have their roots in modernity. These include:

1 The intensification of image production

The increasing invasion of signs and images (in media, display, advertising and so on) into the fabric of everyday life has created a dream world of ideal lifestyles for us to fantasise about and identify with. For example, many commercials are more concerned to attach a sense of lifestyle and experience to the product being sold than to give details about the product itself. Because of this, we get as much satisfaction from consuming the images attached to goods as we do from whatever practical function the goods might serve.

2 The multiplication of cultural mediators

These might include:

- the numerous pundits who populate the media to offer advice on everything from holidays and hair styling to interior design and wine tasting
- the ever growing ranks of popular cultural commentators whose job it is to pick up on all that's new in the worlds of arts, leisure, media and fashion
- the editors of lifestyle magazines
- the makers of television programmes about heritage, architecture, antiques, etc.

- the multiplying range of caring professions, therapists of all kinds, educationalists.

3 The influence of the Bohemian tradition

Many rock musicians, often in bands formed at art school, have tried to make life into a work of art. The earlier work of David Bowie has been one of the most influential examples of this. Many bands and their managers have drawn inspiration for their images, and for the idea of blurring the gap between art and life, from radical artistic subcultures like Dadaism of the 1920s and the Situationists of the 1960s (see Chapter 3 of this book for a brief discussion of Dada, and see Chapter 4 for an overview of what the Situationists aimed at). Punk is often cited to illustrate this influence.

Many musicians also continue the romantic tradition of the aesthetic 'dandy'. Featherstone notes that the rather aristocratic aim of dandyism is to construct an uncompromising public demeanour that is a model of the superior aesthetic lifestyle. A classic example of the art/rock cross-over is the New York band The Velvet Underground: their connections with the pop artist Andy Warhol and the underground New York art scene of the 1960s relate them to both romantic, aristocratic dandyism and trash aesthetics.

Today's pop and rock stars also offer image models, but there is now a huge spectrum of such exemplary lifestyles on offer.

We will have a lot more to say about these changes later, so for now we need only note the fact that many arguably postmodern experiences of identity can be seen as specifically urban ones. It is in the city, for example, that subcultural styles, different tastes and fashions, multiple ethnic influences, and so on, blend and clash most spectacularly.

———— Identity in the city ————

Many postmodern thoughts on identity seem to be addressed specifically to city life. As such, they are built up on ideas about the urban lifestyle which have been present since the early days of the modern metropolis. In this respect the postmodern attitude can be said to amplify rather than radically depart from experiences and conditions which have been in place for over one and a half centuries. Because of this, a lot of recent writing about the postmodern city intensifies themes originally developed by early theorists of modernity.

The beginnings of the modern forms of society noted by Dougas Kellner are usually found in the explosion of large scale urban experience that took place in the middle of the nineteenth century, when over half of the population of England began to live in cities. This soon became the normal course of events as the process of modernisation spread across the world. At the same time a number of writers found that the new city experience highlighted some of the ideas and questions about the self that philosophers had long been exploring. The modern city seemed to live out in concrete terms problems about the relationship between the individual and the collective, for example. With growth of the city there was a new emphasis on the fragmentary and fluid nature of experience. And with this individuals, as we have suggested, became more self-conscious about their way of life, more concerned about their social role, and more anxious about their place in the world.

For example, the French poet Charles Baudelaire, looking at mid-nineteenth-century Paris, suggested that metropolitan consciousness was dominated by a sense of the 'transitory, the fugitive, the contingent'. This picture of the city's fractured and distracted sense of time became for Baudelaire the very essence of modernity. Meanwhile the German sociologist Georg Simmel (1895–1918) more systematically studied how the experience of modernity fragmented the contemporary city-dweller's consciousness of space and time.

This emphasis on the changing nature of how we experience space and time has influenced a number of thinkers concerned with the postmodern world. We will briefly return to this interest in Chapter 8 when we discuss *postmodern geographies*.

Simmel and Baudelaire described an interaction between the metropolis and the mind in which collective solidarity was replaced by a feeling of solitude. In this situation commerce and the industrial state began to intrude too far into human affairs. Simmel pointed out that social bonds between people were now forged by formal institutions, bureaucratic organisations, and money. Money more than anything else was now the anonymous social force which mediated and 'objectified' the relationships between people. This could create a sense of alienation and dehumanisation as people lost their sense of purpose, stability and belonging.

Yet the outcome of all this was, for Simmel, not necessarily completely bleak. On the contrary, he found that the drastic effects of the city could, by increasing people's sense of individuality, enable greater scope for their creative freedom. Although the modern metropolis could bring about a dispiriting feeling of isolation, it could just as easily liberate people from the restrictions of tradition. Simmel argued that although occupants of the modern city become more casual in their ways of life, they are also given a more stimulating, heightened sensitivity to the conditions of their existence. This, for Simmel, was the gateway to greater personal liberty.

Cyberpeople

❝ Into the 1990s the human subject has become a blip: ephemeral, electrically processed, unreal. ❞
(Scott Bukatman, in *Alien Zone,* edited by Annette Kuhn, 1987, page 196)

Over the last few years there has been an explosion of interest in the fusion of human beings and electronic technology implied by the above quote. This interest has been expressed in both cultural studies and scientific publications as well as in movies, computer games, comic books and science fiction novels. Although there are many different variations on the idea of technology–humanity union, and although the phenomenon is far from new, the figure of the 'cyborg' and the current developments of the information superhighway have recently received a great deal of attention.

Films like *Bladerunner* (1982, Director's Cut 1993), *The Terminator* (1984) and *Robocop* (1984) have caught the imaginations of both cinemagoers and cultural commentators. Some have seen these as raising a specifically postmodern set of questions. Giuliana Bruno, for example, finds that '*Bladerunner* posits questions of identity, identification, and history in postmodernism' (in *Alien Zone*, page 193), while Kevin Robins notes that with representations of cyberspace 'we are provided with a virtual laboratory for analysing the postmodern – and perhaps posthuman condition' (in *Cyberspace/Cyberbodies/Cyberpunk*, edited by Featherstone and Burrows 1995, page 140).

Man-machine hybridisation in Shinya Tsukamoto's *Tetsuo*, 1989. BFI Stills, posters and designs.

Boundary confusion

The term *cyborg* (from *cybernetic organism*) was first coined in the 1960s, when it was originally meant to describe the kind of body/ machine combination necessary for humans to endure long periods in outer space. It more generally refers to any machine/human hybrid in which the body and its functions are extended in order to allow better control of its environment, or in which bits of machinery are added to the body in order to improve its performance or extend its life-span. Several commentators have suggested that we are already well on our way to becoming cyborgs in this sense and point to everything from pacemakers, prosthetic body-parts, cosmetic surgery, silicon implants, dialysis machines, test-tube babies and genetic engineering to contact lenses, remote-control handsets and the Internet as proof (and no doubt the list could be much longer than this). However, nowadays it has become common to use the word 'cyborg' to mean just about any recent variation on the old theme of the robot, android or automaton and in the following section I will tend to use the term equally loosely.

Perhaps the most important feature of the cyborg, whether real or fictional, has been its fundamental ambiguity. Many critics have noted that the cyborg either re-draws or eliminates important conceptual boundaries, notably those between mind and body, human and non-human, natural and artificial, inner world and outer world, biological and technological. The cyborgs and replicants in films like *The Terminator* and *Bladerunner* are found to explore in a particularly dramatic and accessible way this boundary confusion. In doing so, they force us to ask questions about how we define terms like 'humanity' and 'selfhood'. In this way cyborgs appear to embody the claims of a number of postmodern theorists. For instance, Jean Baudrillard claims that new technologies have produced new anxieties about what it means to be human:

❢ Am I a man, am I a machine? In the relationship between workers and traditional machines, there is no ambiguity whatsoever. The worker is always estranged from the machine and is therefore alienated by it. He keeps his precious quality of alienated man to himself. Whilst new technology, new machines, new images, interactive screens, do not alienate me at all. With me they form an integrated circuit. ❢

(Quoted in *The Pleasure of the Interface* by Claudia Springer,
Screen 32:2 1991, page 310)

In *Bladerunner*, Harrison Ford's job is to destroy or 'retire' rogue replicants. This is no easy task, however, as replicants are flawless skin jobs – machines which look, act and feel exactly like the real thing. To add to the difficulties, they have emotions and even experience pain. Thus two of the main features we ascribe to 'human-ness' are also found in simulations of human beings. This human quality enables the character Deckard (Ford) to feel attached to Rachel (Sean Young), a skin job who does not even know she is one. By the end of the film – particularly in the later Director's Cut version, where Deckard himself appears to be a replicant – we are left questioning the grounds on which we base our assumptions about what makes people human. As Forest Pyle puts it: 'When we make cyborgs – at least when we make them in movies – we make and, on occasion, unmake our conceptions of ourselves' (*Film Theory Goes to the Movies*, edited by Collins, Radner et. al. 1993 page 228).

How do you differ from a replicant? In what sense are you more than a 'skin job'? It is arguable that with the possibility of artificial intelligence apparently just around the corner such questions have become increasingly urgent.

The next sexual revolution?

In various films, comic books and cyberpunk novels, interacting with computer technology brings about a new kind of human identity. It often involves an escape from the limitations, vulnerabilities and clumsiness of the physical body (cyberpunk writers dismissively call the body 'meat') and into a purer, cybernetic kind of consciousness. A common theme – now particularly appropriate in the AIDS era – is that of imaginary sex. This rather 'pure' notion of sex, involving no physical contact, has been a recurring science fiction dream (or nightmare). We see mental sex in the old Jane Fonda film *Barbarella*, and we see Sylvester Stallone and Sandra Bullock having sex via futuristic headgear in the film *Demolition Man*. Recent developments in virtual reality (including the so-called 'teledildonic' body suit) suggest new forms of hyperreal pornography on the horizon in which you can engage in any kind of fantasy, presumably without fear of bodily harm or arrest.

It has been claimed that in cyberspace we can escape from our real physical selves, become whoever we wish, and experiment with sexual identities at our leisure, unconstrained by the limits of the flesh. In this cybersex revolution we are offered the possibility of performing inside different sexual identities. There is also the chance not only of swapping, but getting outside of gender. This side of cyber-technology has seemed attractive to a number of feminist theorists recently, among them Sadie Plant, Claudia Springer and Donna Haraway.

In her 1985 essay *A Cyborg Manifesto*, Haraway used the figure of the cyborg as a way of imagining a world in which we could transcend the social definitions of masculinity and femininity. It is argued that male-dominated society creates and exploits 'essential' distinctions between male and female in order to keep itself running. But the cyborg, for Haraway, can be seen as a creature in a 'post gender world', which could overstep all socially imposed expectations and constraints. The cybernetic technologies suggest novel ways of getting out of social (and perhaps even biological) limitations on identity by creating new, boundary-blurring images of self. In this way new political alliances can be formed which are no longer restrained by gender, class, sexuality, ethnicity or location.

Sadie Plant has also noted that women can take computer technology from the hands of men and use it to explore alternative forms of fantasised identity which are subversive – if not completely free – of male domination:

> ❝ Like women, software systems are used as man's tools, his media and his weapons; all are developed in the interests of man, but all are poised to betray him . . . Women's liberation is sustained and vitalised by the proliferation and globalisation of software technologies, all of which feed into self-organising systems and enter the scene on her side. ❞

(*Cyberspace/Cyberbodies/Cyberpunk*, edited by Featherstone and Burrows,1995 page 58)

A note of caution

While Plant and Haraway find in cyborg technology the potential to go beyond conventional definitions of gender, it has also been pointed out that the cyberworld does remain largely male-dominated. Although there are signs that a broad spectrum of sexualities other than conventional heterosexual male fantasy has been expressed in cyborg imagery (such as that in comic books and Japanese animated films) much of it still sticks to stereotypical depictions of male and female. It has been suggested that the exaggeration of Arnold Schwarzenegger's signs of masculinity (hard muscles, stern features, etc.) in the *Terminator* films and others are a desperate attempt to hold on to the conventional representations of sexual difference at a time when technology (e.g. genetic engineering) is threatening to make such difference obsolete. A similar point can perhaps be made about the familiar image of the shiny female robot popular in airbrushed science fantasy art, with her Playboy-type features, or the 'ideal woman' created by male teenage computer-geeks in the film *Weird Science* (1985). Add to these examples the growing popularity of pornographic CD-ROMS and it begins to seem that the vision of a pluralistic post-gender cyberworld is still some way off.

Donna Haraway envisages for the cyber-era a new virtual space filled with fluid, fleeting identities. This ideal of a space in which identity is effectively released from all previous social bindings echoes a lot of the postmodern thought we will look at in the rest of this book. It particularly recalls some of the influential thinking of Gilles Deleuze and Felix Guattari, whose work we will consider in the following chapter.

You will never know the real me: Madonna

One of Madonna's early incarnations: *Desperately Seeking Susan*, 1985. BFI Stills, posters and designs.

Of all the superstars who inhabit popular culture, Madonna has attracted a volume of critical interest almost equal to the volume of records, videos and other by-products she has sold. Although no longer generating the kind of fanatical reception accorded her in the 1980s, Madonna still retains that 'aura' which we suggest when we call someone an icon. Whether you personally enjoy Madonna's image and music is not the point. She is an icon, whether you like it or not.

Madonna first came to the attention of the world in the early 1980s, when she put out a series of successful records aimed predominantly at a teenage audience. Nothing about Madonna's early records was particularly unusual in terms of the dance music popular at that time, and as her career developed into the 1990s, she remained firmly within the musical bounds of pop convention. In fact, it is arguable that her records are just one component of the Madonna event, and that her enormous appeal lies at least as much in her media persona as in her music. She has always had a remarkable talent for courting publicity. Many of her concert performances, videos and publications (the 1992 book, *Sex*) have been controversial enough to ensure wide coverage, and so she has maintained a high media presence.

It is often implied that Madonna's status results in large part from the way she wilfully deploys images of (her own ?) sexuality. It seems that as soon as any woman does this, she finds herself in the middle of a fracas, and Madonna has certainly been no exception. People want to know whether she represents a forward or backward step for feminism. They argue about whether Madonna subverts stereotypes or reinforces them.

These are just a couple of the arguments you can have about Madonna, and there are surely many more. But in a chapter of his book *Media Culture* (1995) Douglas Kellner warns against adopting any one polarised view. He argues that the many images Madonna projects of herself defy any attempt to pin her down to a single meaning. He offers an overview of the career-long spectrum of guises in which Madonna has 'imaged' herself, and finds that they only add up to contradiction, multiplicity and enigma. As Madonna herself said of her supposed documentary, *In Bed With Madonna* (a.k.a. *Truth or Dare*, 1991): 'You could watch it and say, I still don't know Madonna, and *good*. Because you will never know the real me.' Not surprisingly, it proves impossible to present the Madonna 'narrative' as a coherent sequence or story of evolution. But a swift glance through the Madonna dossier might remind us of the following milestones:

1978–1986

Madonna first attracts attention as a dancer in Lower East Side New York clubs. First single and album in 1983. First public image: rebellious, exhibitionist, overtly sexual. Clothes are mix-and-match: black lace, black boots, short skirts, chains, buckles, belts, bows, bobby socks, fake pearls, crucifixes. They are teenage, cheap and easily available to the thousands of young women who soon imitate Madonna's brand of street style.

Videos include: *Material Girl* (imitates Marilyn Monroe in *Gentlemen Prefer Blondes*); *Papa Don't Preach* (appears as a teenager with cropped blonde hair); *Open Your Heart* (appears as a stripper in a peep show).

Several changes of hair colour and length, alongside 'flash trash' clothes. Markets 'Boy-Toy' range of Madonna-wear.

Starts her acting career with *Desperately Seeking Susan*.

1986–1989

Begins to display a new, very muscular physique. In videos, mixes male and female dress codes and body language. Regularly puts on a more glamourous and expensive style, often basing her image on silver screen icons like Dietrich and Garbo. Many film roles and stage shows present different versions of Madonna.

1990–present

Justify My Love video makes reference to sadomasochism, homoerotic imagery and bisexuality. Concert performances increase sexual content, with pretend orgies and masturbation. She often wears male clothes. Male dancers in some tours wear dresses and strap-on breasts, while female dancers sport fake penises. Spearheads the vogue for wearing underwear as outerwear. *Blonde Ambition* tour: wears a hard, hi-tech outfit designed by Gaultier, and a hard, hi-tech body. Stirs up the media by publishing a soft-core photo-book presenting herself in stylish, theatrical shots, acting out a polysexual range of fantasies and identities. Claims to be freeing desire and fantasy from guilt. More recently, becomes a torch singer with a fine line in fragile ballads, and the star of *Evita*.

For some critics the whole Madonna phenomenon represents nothing but the worst excesses of commercial exploitation. She is a typical product of cynical media manipulation and her millions of fans are the brain-dead dupes of a vast capitalist conspiracy. Such scorn is not uncommon where popular culture is concerned, and it often gets poured down on the pop music industry with particular spite. Even critics who find something interesting in the way Madonna uses multiple images of sexuality and fantasy sometimes express doubts about her motives. Kellner concedes that many of Madonna's videos are interesting, and even potentially subversive, for how they represent minority points of view. But he finds that her apparently subversive tactics are really just attempts to attract the following of as many segments of the population (e.g. ethnic minorities, gay people, working-class girls, heterosexual men) as possible, and thus to increase sales by having a little of something for everyone. Madonna exploits our culture's objectification of the female body for her own material gain. By presenting herself as a sexual spectacle, she helps to maintain the importance that our sexist culture places on the appearance of women.

Others have seen in Madonna a much more positive role, and have claimed that she offers a powerful model of female assertion and self-sufficiency. They say that instead of being a victim of the system, Madonna is in complete control of her sexuality, uses it in any way she sees fit, and empowers her fans to do the same. Madonna shows that exhibitionism – or making a spectacle of yourself for erotic attention – can be active rather than passive, a skill and not a weakness. It was on these grounds that in 1992 the feminist (or post-feminist) critic Camille Paglia declared Madonna a 'real feminist' for her skill in manipulating and marketing sexuality.

Madonna has been acclaimed for her ability to plunder the conventions of sexual and gender representation, and thus to show them all up as artificial social constructs. In other words, it is argued, she 'de-naturalises' sex and gender and encourages us to play with the constructs in any way we find pleasurable. Madonna's message is that the variety of roles provided by today's culture allows identity to be as plural and playful as you wish. In doing all of this Madonna pushes questions about the politics of identity into a broad public arena in a way that could hardly be achieved by avant-garde art or highbrow theory.

Masks of femininity

Madonna's work can be compared to that of the American artist Cindy Sherman. Sherman first came to the attention of the art world in the late 1970s and early 1980s because of a long series of photographic self-portraits, portraying herself in a seemingly endless array of cinematic guises. Each of this sequence of black and white photographs, called simply *Untitled Film Stills*, presented Sherman as a filmic 'type' of femininity, and in doing so played on the viewer's skill in interpreting media images. An understanding, however unconscious, of how styles of lighting, dress, and posture create meaning within our culture enabled the viewer to instantly, if sometimes dimly, identify the images. These were at once specific and generic, in that you could rarely name the source, but could almost intuitively recognise the type: Hitchcockian heroines, muses from half-remembered French art movies, femmes fatales, nice girls, troubled teenagers, traumatised adolescents from stalk 'n' slash thrillers, and so on through dozens of starring roles in stills from imaginary movies.

As is the case with Madonna, Sherman appeared to be playing with multiple images of 'female-ness'. As you travelled from one photo to another either in a book or exhibition of her work, this produced an unsettling effect: you were aware that these were self-portraits and that they were therefore of Cindy Sherman. But the photos had an obvious staged quality (they were scenes from mock movies and not slices of life), and it was clear from the start that Sherman was working with stereotypes rather than attempting to offer a simple picture of her inner, private world. In what sense was self-portraiture a suitable description of this? What was the relationship between public, mass-produced images of femininity and Sherman's real self? Did the very multiplicity of images suggest that her self was multiple or fragmented? Or did the nature of 'her' self no longer come into the question?

Madonna hoped that we would never know the real her. Similarly the cumulative effect of all Sherman's roles on the viewer is often the sense that the more images pile up, the further you get from the real Cindy Sherman. No matter how far you try to go in search of her you will always be confronted by another mask.

Changing faces

In a review first published in the journal *Screen* in 1983, Judith Williamson found that Sherman's photographs reminded her of a certain sartorial dilemma. She likened trying to decide what clothes to wear before going out in the morning (if only my wardrobe was as well stocked as Williamson's seems to be!) to selecting a personality. How we are understood is partly dependent on how we appear. What we put on, how we do our hair, what gestures we make, all make us appear to be certain types of person. Whatever outfit we wear lends us one particular identity, which excludes others. And yet we really do not have to be fixed to any one such public identity. We can have any number of them at our disposal, can revel in our ability to 'speak' through any number of (dis)guises. Williamson observes, for example, that if she wears a little leather skirt she will be defined in one particular way, and that if she wears a smart suit another set of connotations will come into play. Each way of appearing can define you as you occupy particular social spaces, but it will fail to hint at all of the different 'yous' you can have: the sensible two-piece you wear in your high-powered job may, for your audience, firmly locate you in the stereotype of business-like-person-who-likes-to-get-things-done, but this hardly speaks of the alley-cat you turn into on a Friday night. As Williamson puts it 'often I have wished I could . . . appear simultaneously in every outfit, just to say, how dare you think any one of these is *me*. But also, see, I can be all of them' (*Consuming Passions*,1986, page 91). In the postmodern world you do not have to be pinned down to a single image of self.

Self-defence

Williamson's description of how you can toy with multiple identities depends very much on manipulating how the public sees you: other people deduce things about you from your appearance and this tends to project stereotypical identities on to you. The art critic Craig Owens has noted that this process has a particular resonance for women, since, according to him, women live under 'the masculine desire to fix the woman in a stable and stabilising identity'.

But Williamson notes that Sherman's self portraits demand to be seen as throwing the repertoire of feminine identities 'back where they belong, in the recognition of the beholder.' They suggest that women can avoid being objectified at the hands of masculine desire by overstating or ironically adopting the pool of masks at their disposal. This is a form of self-defence against male surveillance, and we can perhaps see it in Madonna as well.

(The idea of feminine masquerade hinted at here has recently been explored by a number of feminist theorists. These have been informed especially by the French psychoanalytic thinker Luce Irigaray. Some feminist film theorists, such as Mary Anne Doane, have often found the idea of masquerade useful.)

So Sherman and Madonna are relevant to the postmodern approach to the self because they make all identities appear equally artificial, including gender. They do not suggest that you can easily step outside of the social definitions of identity. Instead they show that culture provides a multitude of images of self and that the ability to combine these into new configurations creates a 'play of signs' in which you can construct an empowering sense of individuality.

Although Madonna and Sherman can therefore be seen as upsetting some of the stereotypes perpetuated by mass media, they do not do this through a tactic of elitist rejection: instead of presenting themselves in a superior way as overthrowing popular culture or refusing to play its games, they deliberately work on what it makes available and, especially in Madonna's case, do so on its own terms. To this extent they are both postmodern artists in the way I described in Chapter 3.

—— Identity as construction ——

By discussing some of the work of Madonna and Sherman, we have begun to see a questioning of the relationship between public and private models of identity. This questioning suggests that the connection between your inner self and the outer appearance you show to the world is not simply a relationship of expression. In other words, your public identity does not simply express what you are really like, deep down.

By the same token, some postmodernist versions of the self suggest that there is no 'deep down' to identity: the fact that Madonna and Sherman adopt so many different images suggests that there may not be a single true self that resides beneath them all. No matter how deep you go, another surface is all you get

These reflections can be formulated as postmodernism's *anti-essentialist* or *constructionist* views of identity.

Anti-essentialism

This is opposition to the idea that people have a timeless, universal core which ultimately explains their actions. Anti-essentialism has been a hotly debated topic within recent feminist work, where it has often seemed necessary to stress the idea of gender as a cultural and not a natural or essential category. Given that attempts are sometimes made to define women's 'proper' place in terms of what is supposedly natural it has become important to dispute the way society habitually calls upon an idea of 'nature' as the ultimate explanation of things which happen within culture. The work of Judith Butler (e.g. *Gender Trouble*) is a good, challenging example of work in this area. Similar themes of anti-essentialism have been debated in relation to gay politics and in relation to ideas of racial or ethnic identity.

Constructionism

There are really two versions of this:

- Instead of being born with a particular in-built substance, we *become* what we are through being acted on by a series of social factors. You are constructed by the social and are ultimately determined by it.

- We can more or less freely fabricate our identities for ourselves. We have a degree of choice about how to represent ourselves.

You can see that these two versions of constructionism are in considerable tension with one another. For this reason, arguments over postmodernist accounts of the self often end up repeating the old philosophical debate about free will versus determinism. We do not have to enter that debate. If you side with either one of these versions of the constructed self to the total exclusion of the other, you are likely to end up in theoretical hot water. For our purposes it is safe to say that personal identity is formed out of the tension between the two, and that this tension can manifest itself in different ways as we enter different circumstances. A truly postmodern approach would reject any attempt at a single, unified and universal theory of selfhood and would look instead at how the determined and the free versions of self construction interact with and affect each other in variable ways according to our changing social situations.

The presentation of self

In trying to sketch new conceptions of self identity, theorists of postmodernism inevitably borrow from various sources. In some cases this involves re-examining older theorists through the lens of present concerns and claiming them to be postmodernists ahead of their time. One such theorist is the American sociologist Erving Goffman. Goffman is seen as an important precursor of the postmodern self because he studied people not in terms of what they were 'inside', but in terms of how they performed in social situations. The important text here is his 1959 book, *The Presentation of Self in Everyday Life*. In this book Goffman studied how people react to one another in concrete social circumstances. In doing so, he was working within established sociological terms, and to this extent his work should not be seen as unique. However, his work seems to have caught the contemporary imagination because of his insistence on the centrality of what he called 'image management' to our lives. Goffman studied the various institutions that make up social life (e.g. the workplace, high school) from what he called a 'dramaturgical' perspective: mainly concerned with how people act out social roles in particular circumstances, Goffman saw life as essentially theatrical. In his book, life is divided into 'on stage' and 'back stage' moments, and people are called 'actors'.

Goffman tended to have no time for 'modernist' questions about whether the self was authentic or not. His only interest was in whether our various performances successfully promote our social survival. Hence the self 'is not an organic thing that has a specific location, whose fundamental fate is to be born, to mature, and to die; it is a dramatic effect arising diffusely from a scene that is presented, and the characteristic issue, the crucial concern, is whether it will be credited or discredited' (page 223).

So Goffman writes of the self as a series of facades erected before different audiences. These facades only *appear* to emanate from some intrinsic self inside the social performer. In fact, the self is an effect, and not a cause, of the facade. It is also not something you individually own. It arises from interaction with other actors on the social stage. Hence you are 'a peg on which something of a collaborative manufacture will be hung for a while', as Goffman puts it.

In an essay of 1992 (in the journal *Theory, Culture and Society* Vol. 9), Efrat Tseelon claims Goffman for postmodernism. Goffman's emphasis on the 'facade self', fits in well with the view of postmodern culture as a world full of flat images and simulations (see our discussion of Jean Baudrillard's work in Chapter 4, for example). In this world it is impossible to distinguish in any simple way the real from the artificial. Nor is it possible to see selves as independent individuals with essences which they then express in whatever ways they personally prefer. In postmodernism, by Tseelon's account, the idea of a real or deep self vanishes, and is replaced with a superficial collage of social constructs. Goffman can then be seen as offering an early picture of this postmodern transition.

Summary

Postmodernism suggests in various ways that self identity is something fabricated 'on the outside'. We saw this with Madonna, with Cindy Sherman, and with Judith Williamson's quandary about what 'identity' to wear each day. All implied that appearance and behaviour *produce* the self as well as *express* it.

Your identity is a fabrication that you can manipulate more or less at will. Even your sexuality can be something you *have* or *do* rather than something you *are*. Your identity is made on the surface through what you do and how you display yourself: as the British critic Angela McRobbie has said of Madonna, she constructs herself as 'all body'.

So the visions of the postmodern self looked at in this chapter say that you are a play of surfaces, a set of shifting signs. You have no single essential self beneath all the faces you show to the world, because you are scattered over a complex network of social forces.

These ideas can be regarded as forming a specifically postmodern picture of identity on at least two grounds:

• They pose a challenge to the modernist view of individuals as independent, individual sources for the expression of unique insights. We will discuss this in more detail in the following chapter.

• The growing complexity of life under conditions of social postmodernity brings about a greater awareness of the various social roles and identities offered to us in consumer culture. There is in this way an acceleration of the demands on the notion of the self that were made in modernity. Hence the idea of the postmodern self plays a part in, and enters us into, general discussion about new ways of living in our society.

7

IDENTITY CRISIS PART 2

This chapter goes into a little more detail about some of the ideas which have contributed to what is now thought of as the postmodern view of identity and selfhood. This should add further conceptual 'meat' to the postmodernised self of popular culture, cities and cyber-scapes which we discussed in the previous section. It will also pave the way for some of the thoughts on the so-called *postmodern politics of difference* which follows in the concluding chapter.

Michel Foucault: the invention of man

Discussions about the self in postmodernism are often conducted with reference to the work of Michel Foucault (1926–1984). Foucault wrote elaborate histories of social institutions as diverse as the penal system, psychiatry and the social sciences. He believed that no such institutions were neutral or independent, and argued that it was an important political task to examine how they were tied in to the complex operations of power in our society. This power was exercised through surveillance, monitoring and other forms of regulation of people's lives.

For Foucault, the modern-day notion of the self is bound up with, and inseparable from, the workings of such structures and institutions, and so none of us can claim to stand apart from the exercise of power. But, as we will see, Foucault does not provide a theory of how naturally free human individuals are oppressed from above by the laws of any one dominant class or group. Instead he proposes that humanity is simply an idea and that, like any other idea, it has a history: 'the archaeology of our thinking demonstrates clearly that man is a recent invention, perhaps also approaching his end'. To approach Foucault's often demanding work there are at least two heavily used terms that you need to grasp. These are *the subject* and *discourse*.

The subject

Within much postmodern theory, and within the critical tradition from which it often draws (notably structuralism and poststructuralism: see Chapter 5), *people* do not come into the picture very often. In this body of work, the *person* is often replaced by the *subject*.

In day-to-day speech, when we talk of being 'subjective', we mean that we are basing our ideas on personal experience, that we are seeing things from our own point of view, and perhaps that our ideas reveal a certain amount of prejudiced self-interest. This is close to one definition of the subject simply as a thinking and feeling, conscious self.

As Kaja Silverman points out in her book *The Subject of Semiotics* (1983), this taken-for-granted idea of the individual can be dated back to the Renaissance, where it came to designate individual consciousness as a private, essentially free, decision-making agent and source of meaning. The Renaissance idea of the individual 'man' assumed that 'he' was an independent, fixed entity, a 'human nature' clear of historical and cultural circumstances. This gave birth to the romantic idea that humanity can achieve a transcendent state of truth to nature through philosophy, religion and art. This is, of course, the stuff of popular culture as well. Most films, for example, are about the triumph of the will, the struggle of the individual against the collective, the necessity of being true to yourself, and so forth. Whether such representations of the self can be a positive factor does not appear to have been of particular interest to Foucault, however. He would prefer to ask questions like: why have these views of the self arisen at this point in history? Where do they come from? How do they relate to the distribution of power in society?

The idea of subjectivity (i.e. being a 'subject') has been applied in many different ways by different theorists and so it cannot be said to have a single meaning. Generally speaking though, as theorists like

Foucault use the term, a subject means not simply a conscious person, but a specifically social fact, a being which is at least partially *subjected* to socially produced constraints and divisions. Thus Foucault tends to deny the subject any internal substance. For him the distinction between public and private selves implied by 'human nature' is a false or at least irrelevant one. The subject cannot be reduced to individual consciousness; there are only practices or techniques of the self.

For Foucault, definitions of the self are given only in the social relations we live by. The self is political and knowledge of it is connected to power.

Discourse

Like the subject, *discourse* can have many different meanings according to who is using it. While it can sometimes designate little more than a general realm of representations, it more often refers to specific social institutions and disciplines. So we might speak of the discourse of literary criticism, for example, because literary criticism is both a particular way of putting language to use (e.g. writing criticism) and a discipline (literature) formed within a particular institution (academia). Discourse as Foucault tends to mean it involves all aspects equally – the institution, the discipline, and the language use all go together. One enables the other.

Discourses can be seen as controlled systems for the production of knowledge. Though regulated, they are not completely closed systems and have to allow for change and limited dissent. For example, literary critics will disagree over the quality of a particular poem or the meaning of a particular play, but this will not threaten the discourse of literary criticism itself. Indeed, such internal disagreements are crucial in keeping the discourse up and running. Nevertheless, discourses put a limit on what is sayable at any one time: they define what counts as 'legitimate' or 'illegitimate' statements.

Foucault sees discourses everywhere. They are the very stuff of society and they mediate all aspects of life. But discourse is not just an abstract public sphere of words and images; it exists in concrete social situations and has very real effects. One such discourse is psychology. As Henriques, Hollway et al. argue in their book *Changing the Subject* (1984), psychology has played a part in our current 'common sense' views of the self and its relation to society.

Psychology produces individuals as its objects of enquiry, and in doing so contributes to the impression that individuals need to be enquired into. The only reason for embarking on such an enquiry, in the Foucaultian view, is to keep humanity in check, to prevent 'deviants' from upsetting the social order, and to regulate people so that they can become 'useful' members of society.

In his studies of the institution of the mental hospital (e.g. *Madness and Civilisation*), Foucault looks at how professional discourse employs 'scientific' knowledge to make distinctions between the sane and the insane, the normal and the abnormal. Other discourses make distinctions regarding what counts as acceptable behaviour. For example, we distinguish between legal and illegal killing, or between proper and improper sexual conduct. These judgements (Foucault calls them 'dividing practices') are always historically particular, variable from culture to culture, and subject to change.

Conclusion

Society defines itself by what it excludes. By defining and marginalising groups of 'deviants' as criminal, mad or ill, it reassures itself of its own sanity, health and naturalness. Thus discourses are the systems of exclusion and categorisation upon which society depends. We all participate in these systems.

—————— Let's talk about sex ——————

We are used to thinking of modern society as something which causes us to repress our instinctive sexual desires. The demands of modern life, its laws and its censorship all conspire to keep our sexual liberty under lock and key. We harbour all manner of dark desires, but the conventions of the modern world prevent us from releasing them. This repression causes misery and even illness. Discovering your true sexuality can bring fulfilment and liberty.

This is what Foucault, in his three-volume *History of Sexuality* (English Editions 1980–1986), dismissively calls 'the repressive hypothesis'. He believes that the widespread idea of repression is something of a myth. He argues that, far from being repressive of sexuality, modern western society actually produces sexuality in the form of endless sex-talk, sex-study and sex-theory. Rather than being silenced, sex since the supposedly repressed Victorian age has grown in importance, and become a serious object of study. It has become the subject on most people's lips. The discourse on sex is ever growing.

It is not hard to see Foucault's point. People often remark that our culture is obsessed with sex. Many popular films make a feature of sex, many products advertise themselves through sex appeal, Sunday news-papers are always carrying the latest 'sensational' findings of sex surveys, advice columns are pre-occupied with sex, sexual hang-ups are the stock-in-trade of the endless experts who plug their books on talk shows, sexologists make small fortunes out of discovering new ways of achieving orgasms, and so on. Add to these much more serious issues, like the promotion of safe sex in the light of AIDS, well-publicised debates about homosexuality in the armed forces, widespread media concern about the sex life of adolescents, documentaries and news items about sex crimes, their perpetrators and their victims, and it becomes clear that culture is indeed saturated by discourses of sexuality.

On one level, we could call this 'only natural' but for Foucault, the question of the 'natural' is of marginal relevance at best. He argues that the discourse on sexuality is a modern phenomenon which serves only to create the impression that there is such a thing as 'natural' sex.

You could also say that all this sex-discourse is a healthy sign on the road to sexual freedom and enlightenment. But again, says Foucault, you would be mistaken: it is just another form of social control:

> ❢ All this garrulous attention which has us in a stew over sexuality, is it not motivated by one basic concern . . . to constitute a sexuality that is economically useful and politically conservative? ❢
>
> (*The Foucault Reader*, edited by P. Rabinow 1984, (page 317).

Discourse does not free sex: it invents it. Discussion and examination do not liberate sexuality: they make it into a problem. This is because the discourse on sexuality creates the notion that sex is an absolute, abstract category. Sex and sexuality have become the titles used to cover all bodies and their pleasures. The concept 'sex' is now the basic drive which motivates all of human life, a dark secret, a deep mystery.

So it is no longer enough to simply create bodily pleasures for their own sake. All bed-time (or anywhere, anytime) activities are now sexualised, in the sense that they are seen as manifestations of a single, sexual foundation common to all of humanity. All bodily pleasures are now understood in terms of the degree to which they deviate from, conform to, improve, or avoid sex. Sex is the dominant term, the standard against which 'the body and pleasure' are measured.

And in our own society it is heterosexuality which provides this standard. Homosexuality, some 'aberrant' sexual practices, and so on, might be tolerated, but they are still identified by their difference from the heterosexist norm. The presence of this norm enables society to marginalise some sexual practices as 'against nature', and thereby to prove the naturalness of the heterosexual monogamy and family values upon which mainstream society bases itself.

Yet despite all this Foucault avoids the model of 'sexuality versus repressive society'. He paradoxically notes instead that the discourse on sex can actually encourage sexual diversity:

❦ The 'putting into discourse of sex', far from undergoing a process of restriction, on the contrary has been subjected to a mechanism of increasing incitement . . . the techniques of power exercised over sex have not obeyed a principle of rigorous selection, but rather one of dissemination and implantation of polymorphous sexualities. ❧

(*The Foucault Reader*, edited by Paul Rabinow, 1984 page 300)

In other words sex discourse 'discovers' and classifies an ever expanding encyclopaedia of preferences, gratifications and perversions. It creates a realm of perversion by discovering, commenting on and exploring it. It brings it into being as an object of study, and in doing so serves to categorise and objectify those who occupy what has been made into the secret underworld of 'deviance'. People no longer own their pleasures: they become specimens of well-documented sexual types (a 'new specification of individuals') instead. Our sexuality and our selves have been turned into a problem, and by constantly encouraging us to talk about it, the discourse on sexuality ropes us into looking for the solution: 'We must . . . ask why we burden ourselves today with so much guilt for having once made sex a sin.' (*The Foucault Reader* page 297)

Pleasures of resistance/resistance to pleasure

All of this may begin to sound a little too Big-Brotherish, but Foucault does allow for gaps in the working of discourses. He argues that wherever you find discourse you also find a conflict between those who control it (i.e. who place a limit on what can and cannot be said) and those who have been denied the right to representation through it. Wherever you find suppression, you also find subversion: no matter how frightening a particular regime may be people always find possibilities for resistance. In fact, the two go hand in hand: without subversion, society would have nothing to suppress, without suppression, there would be nothing to subvert. Certain disobedient sexual practices (for example S&M or bondage) might therefore be seen as the result, and not simply the victim, of oppression. Foucault calls this a spiralling 'double impetus' of power to pleasure, pleasure to power.

--------------- **Summary** ---------------

Our humanist picture of individuality is a product of modern western systems of knowledge. These came into being with the birth of the human sciences in the age of the Enlightenment and Foucault has no interest in whether they are capable of producing a positive effect on individual lives. His concern is with how they feed into potentially oppressive ideas about the self which we still hold on to today. Modern discourses like psychiatry, criminology and sexology are 'dividing practices' which objectify and categorise us and thus fundamentally affect our experience of personal and social identity.

The deconstructed self: Jacques Lacan

Jacques Lacan (1901–81) was a psychoanalytic theorist and practitioner whose work was engaged in re-treading Sigmund Freud (the founder of psychoanalysis) in the light of contemporary theory. He believed that Freud offered fundamental insights into the life of the mind, but that the time in which he was writing prevented him from realising the truly radical nature of his own theories and discoveries.

Freud

Freud had provided the basic texts of psychoanalysis and had fur-nished the field will many of its central terms. In Freud's work (for example *The Interpretation of Dreams*, 1900) the present mental state of clients was rooted in the lost events of infancy – events which it was the job of the psychoanalyst to uncover. For Freud, the family unit was the primary site of numerous dramas and conflicts which influenced the shape of the mental structure. Despite his emphasis on the family (and thus to a certain extent the self) as a social formation, many of Freud's theories were ultimately grounded in biological mod-els. The infant was born as an incoherent mass of naturally occurring basic instincts. Infantile dramas like breast-feeding and weaning off served to 'write over' and channel biological drives and appetites, and in doing so they transformed the child from pure biological organism to conscious social being. Put simply, Freud's work chronicles the con-flicts in the psyche between instinctual and cultural forces. He finds that although we attempt to keep a lid on our unconscious natural drives, they keep 'accidentally on purpose' bubbling to the surface in day-to-day life in the form of dreams, jokes, slips of the tongue, verbal tics and other seemingly insignificant little human events.

Lacan

Lacan retains the Freudian framework but shakes it up considerably. He rejects all popular attempts to explain Freudian ideas, and takes from those ideas a model of mental life which is full of fracture and internal conflict. Where Freud (at least in the 'tamed' versions of his thinking adopted by many of his followers) suggested that the con-flicts of mental life could be resolved, Lacan saw them as fundamen-tally irreparable: discord and fracture cannot be cleared away from the psyche because they *are* the psyche. Lacan therefore thought that the potential radicalism of Freud was hindered by the way he often resorted to permanent, universal drives as the underlying cause of mental disturbances. Lacan deflects attention away from this stress on supposedly natural causes and claims that psychoanalysis should take an almost anthropological interest in the cultural.

Language

Less emphasis should be put on the idea that self-sufficient events within the individual mind are the source of dreams, word-associations, Freudian slips and so on, as these are affected primarily by cultural rather than personal factors. Hence Freudian slips, for example, are an effect of words as much as they are the product of one person's unconscious drives. Heavily influenced by the structuralist theories of language and representation which we discussed in Chapter 5, Lacan claimed that the unconscious was structured like language.

Biology can tell us little. The unconscious is by definition unknowable, and can only be 'reconstructed' in language. The words of the client in analysis cannot act like windows into the depths of the unconscious. The analyst does not so much see through the client's words as engage in an act of reading: he or she interprets dream imagery (as described by the client in words) or a stream of word associations in much the same way as he or she would read any other kind of writing. Psychoanalysis can therefore learn much from linguistics and should look harder at the linguistic processes involved in reading and speaking. The unconscious, for Lacan, manifests itself in the way words fail to work. Thus the client in effect speaks the unconscious into being.

The mirror-stage

Lacan's vision of the self is outlined in his famous essay, *The Mirror Stage as Formative of the Function of the I*, first published in 1949 (from a lecture on *The Looking-glass Phase,* originally presented in 1936). In it he describes how, as infants, we gain a deluded sense of self-identity via identification with images and reflections.

In our first months of infancy we are in disarray. We have no co-ordination, we cannot control our bodily functions and we experience ourselves as a bunch of ill-fitting spare parts (Lacan calls this infant an 'hommelette': a scrambled little man). But in the mirror stage, which occurs at the age of six to eighteen months, the infant sees its own behaviour reflected in the gestures of adults and other children and in mirrors. Fascinated by this reflection, the child (mis)recognises itself as a whole entity for the first time. It sees an image of itself as a unified person, an image which promises for the child that it will soon achieve full co-ordination of its body. The incoherent 'hommelette' sees an image of itself as an independent being and learns to identify with this image. This is when the ego (the sense of yourself as an individual) is formed.

Thus your sense of self is fundamentally bound up with an 'exterior' image. Instead of simply coming from within, your identity is formed out of a situation in which you see yourself for the first time from the outside. For Lacan this means that alienation and division are built into your identity from the outset. The result in adult life is that you are in a constant but fruitless state of desire for some mythical inner unity and stability to match the unity and stability you thought you saw in your childhood reflection. We spend our lives trying (and failing) to make ourselves 'whole'.

So Lacan thinks that Freudian psychoanalysis has clung for too long to supposedly permanent fixtures of the self. Selfhood is really nothing but a fleeting, unstable, incomplete and open-ended mess of desires which cannot be fulfilled. Hence 'Man cannot aim at being whole. The 'total personality' is another of the deviant premises of modern psychotherapy' (*Ecrits: a Selection*, English Edition 1977 page 223).

The dispersed subject

In 1972 the Foucault-influenced philosopher Gilles Deleuze and the Lacan-influenced psychoanalyst Felix Guattari collaborated on a book called *Anti-Oedipus: Capitalism and Schizophrenia*. In that book they championed a world of fragmentation and flux in which individuals were liberated from any 'repressive' notions about the rationality, unity, or stability of the self. Because of this emphasis, the book is now often considered a major early statement of a postmodern position on identity and society.

The politics of desire

Like Michel Foucault (see above), Deleuze and Guattari were concerned with the power relationship between modern society and desire. They claimed that the institutions and discourses of modernity were a soft kind of fascism which exercised dominance by inserting repression into all aspects of everyday existence. Under modernity's capitalist system, repression and dominance were not so much forced on to people as lived by them.

In this respect, Deleuze and Guattari worked out their ideas within a very particular radical intellectual framework. As well as Foucault's work on how subjects and their pleasures are defined and controlled by the institutions of the modern state, we could also point to Guy Debord and the Situationists (see Chapter 4) as influences. Rather like Deleuze and Guattari, they believed that capitalism had infiltrated all of existence, and had taken away from people the possibility of experiencing genuine freedom, expression and satisfaction. All desires under capitalism were 'false', 'mediated' desires.

Their work is also related to that of the Frankfurt School of critical theory. Two books associated with this group of critics are:

One-dimensional Man (1964) by Herbert Marcuse

Marcuse was deeply suspicious of the way modernity had expanded communication technologies and consumerism into our lives, and saw them as central to a new, more insidious kind of totalitarianism which – through the production of 'false needs' – sought to penetrate consciousness itself, neutralise all voices of dissent, and turn us all into interchangeable components of the capitalist machine.

Dialectic of Enlightenment (1944) by Theodor Adorno and Max Horkheimer

Adorno and Horkheimer pessimistically believed that even in supposedly democratic societies (America was singled out), mass culture acted as an authoritarian force which reduced people to passive social conformity. As far as they were concerned, all of mass culture injects the capitalist status quo into people's unconscious, making its victims lose their individuality, and persuades them to willingly accept its values.

Deleuze and Guattari's work was related to the above through what they called *territorialisation*. This they defined as the process by which both society and theory (particularly Freudian and Marxist theory) attempted to tame human desire. Capitalist systems territorialise desire and creativity by channelling them into organised social areas (or codes) such as consumerism, finance, the law, psychiatry, the nuclear family unit, social class and conventional gender roles. Capitalist systems effectively control desire by attaching it to the production and consumption of goods, and by trapping social subjects in an organised network of normalising impersonal social structures and processes. This concern with the effects of the 'rational' and anonymous systems of modern society in some respects recalls the work of earlier sociologists of modernity on the growth of the urbanised ways of life (see for example the short section on Georg Simmel in the previous chapter). But what give Deleuze and Guattari their own particular flavour, and what have recently caught the eye of postmodernism, are their attacks on both Marxism and orthodox psychoanalysis.

Arguing with Marxism

In spite of their interest in how capitalism territorialises human life, and in trying to formulate a revolutionary theory, Deleuze and Guattari make a point of parting company with central aspects of Marxism (and Marxist-derived schools of thought like the Frankfurt School).

Where Marxism emphasised social class as the site of oppression and eventual revolution Deleuze and Guattari see the unity of the working class as a myth which suppresses diversity. For example, women, students and/or ethnic groups are often pushed by Marxists to the edges of class struggle, or are blanketed over by the single, all-embracing category of class. Rejecting this hierarchy, Deleuze and Guattari argue that social class is just one of the many lines along which both oppression and disobedience can run. Class struggle is just one strand in social life, rather than the basis of it.

Although it constantly tries to regulate all aspects of life, capitalism has the effect of undoing identity by channelling desires in many different directions at once. It continually destabilises itself by inventing new territories for consumer desire. As commodities multiply, there are more things to desire, more images to identify with, and more lines of escape. Learning to live this proliferation of contradictory desires and identifications offers us paths for liberation and defiance. By becoming intense, 'decentred' consumers, we can pose a threat to the territorialisation of private and social life.

So unlike the members of the Frankfurt school, Deleuze and Guattari did not picture the state as a single, monolithic agency. They did not see capitalism as automatically successful in its attempts to produce sameness and conformity. Indeed, against Adorno and Horkheimer's view of the capitalist system as enforced homogenisation, Deleuze and Guattari believed that capitalism could generate more and more multiplicity, and that it therefore actually contains the seeds of revolution.

Arguments with Freudianism

Deleuze and Guattari also took issue with some of the founding claims of psychoanalysis. They argued that 'establishment' psychoanalysis (including Jacques Lacan: see above) reduced all of life to the single structure of the nuclear family.

Freud and his followers focused almost exclusively on conflicts in the mother-child-father relationship as the centre and base of all subsequent psychological conditions. Every mental event in adult life was connected to infantile desires formed in this triangular relationship. Deleuze and Guattari saw this as a serious reduction of the complexity of desire as it is experienced in the present. Freudianism takes the family as a pre-given, universal category. Issues of class, location or race, for example, do not come into it: all families act on the unconscious in essentially the same way, with nothing to do with social conditions or history. It does not matter to Freudianism whether the father is a miner, a banker, a trade unionist, or is unemployed. It does not matter whether the family live in a slum or a palace. Whether the parents are from different ethnic or religious backgrounds is neither here nor there. And if Freud were writing today, he would probably have little interest in what films the family members watched, what records they listened to or what magazines they read (except in so far as these could be said to express some underlying unconscious cause). None of these would fundamentally affect the essential mother-child-father triangle. In short, Freud takes politics and culture out of the family. So Deleuze and Guattari argued that the analysis of individual identity should be pushed outside of the narrow confines of 'mommy, daddy and me', and into a much wider social terrain.

Thanks to the popularisation of Freudian ideas (in Hitchcock films and dream interpretation manuals, for example), we are used to imagining an unconscious core lying deep within our minds, insulated from the world. Social roles, politics and public events are frequently understood to be things which influence us on various mental levels, but which do not penetrate deep down into this unconscious core. The unconscious has effects on us, but itself remains untouched.

By contrast, Deleuze and Guattari propose that your unconscious is constantly 'rewritten' by society and history, endlessly remade through direct contact with the outside world. It lives in the present.

One of the effects of Freudianism is the rather widely held belief that people's consumption habits can be explained by something in their unconscious. It might be claimed, for example, that if I happened to be an avid consumer of violent horror videos, the mystery of my enthusiasm could be solved by reference to a long-lost potty-training incident, repressed incestuous desires, my never having passed successfully through the oral stage of infantile development, or (most likely) castration anxiety. Thus the 'answer' would be sought in my supposedly secret past, and hopefully I could be cured.

But from Deleuze and Guattari's perspective such a view would seriously undervalue the complexity of my viewing (dis)pleasures as they are expressed in the present. For I am not simply wired into a closed-circuit relationship between myself, my video-recorder and some long forgotten 'primal scene'. You also have to take into account the relationships (and the differences) between the (dis)pleasures provided by video nasties and the (dis)pleasures I also gain from French art-house movies, Busby Berkeley spectaculars, spaghetti Westerns, kitchen sink dramas, and so on.

But you would also have to consider my entire social field: the jobs I do, the people I know, the kind of person I would like to be, the kind of person I would like not to be, the magazines and books I read, the places I shop . . .

In addition to all of these things, you would surely have to look at the social and technological conditions which enabled the video-player to come into being; the conditions of production and distribution in the low-budget exploitation film industry; the role of censorship and, in some cases, the prohibition of certain films in creating the desire for forbidden viewing, and any number of characteristics of the social and cultural traditions of western society that my films participate in.

The point is that none of these factors are really marginal to my consumer desire. Indeed, in Deleuze and Guattari's work, there is no distinction to be made between the centre and the margin. What we have instead is a free-floating network of relationships, interweavings, cross-fertilisations and undercuttings. No unified unconscious entity occupies the centre of, or 'masters', this network. Thus, rather than express a single subjective secret meaning, my consumer desires are articulated and generated through and across a web of 'social flows'.

So Deleuze and Guattari argue that subjectivity should be seen as extended through or dispersed over the many complex circuits of culture and society: the unconscious 'partakes of the spread of signs from the most disparate social and material flows'. From this point of view unconscious wishes and appetites do not simply belong to you as a result of personal experience. They are public: they are constantly produced and reproduced in concrete social conditions and experience.

Desiring machines

Where Freudianism has tended to represent the unconscious as a dark and dangerous but also fixed and unchanging force, it is seen by Deleuze and Guattari as a 'desiring machine'.

'Desire' is vaguely defined by Deleuze and Guattari as a kind of creative energy, ceaselessly renewing itself and causing chaos. Imagine a reasonably benign hybrid of *The Thing* in John Carpenter's film of that name, the morphing T1000 in *Terminator 2* and the Borg in *Star Trek: the Next Generation,* and you get something close to Deleuze and Guattari's conception of desire. The dynamic force behind all social and personal actions and interactions, desire constantly flows into multiple, random connections with people and objects. It constantly spills over the territorial boundaries which modern social structures keep trying to force it into. A mercurial, ever-adaptable energy, desire is revolutionary to Deleuze and Guattari because it always seeks to transcend limits, and has no time for repressive concerns about usefulness, productivity or efficiency.

─────────── **Summary** ───────────

Deleuze and Guattari:

- see the idea of stable identities as a harmful illusion and celebrate difference, chaos, and the ongoing process of change as the only liberation, and focus on the need to bring the multiplicity of our desires into being

- reject the idea that the psyche is naturally whole, unified, or coherent

- deny the possibility of providing a total or universal theory of the psyche in general

- propose an approach in which 'pure difference' reigns, and cannot be reduced to underlying foundations or essences

- see the self as a flux of desires and 'intensities' which both shoot out in many directions and absorb many influences

- argue that the production and circulation of desire in society is more important to an understanding of identity than needs or instincts.

In the postmodern view your subjectivity is seen as a kind of hybrid of different social codes and ideologies which bear on race, social class, family, age, location and gender. Who or what you are at any one point in time comes from the way these different discourses act out processes of conflict and combination within you. Although you are always socially defined, you are not necessarily stuck with just one such definition: changes in the self can come about as these different factors engage in many-levelled interactions and jostle for domination over each other.

A criticism

James M. Glass has expressed deep reservations about what he calls the postmodern celebration of shattered selves. He argues that in picturing the self as socially defined and multiple, postmodern theory empties identity of all meaning and substance. This, he says, is an irresponsible and ill-informed thing to do. In celebrating fracture, conflict and process within the formation of identity, postmodernism makes a number of mistakes.

It fails to take seriously enough the fact that for many people the supposedly postmodern attributes of subjectivity are experienced in a painful way. What is the use of arguing, as some postmodernists do, that there is no real tension between the inner and outer self, when for many people the experience of conflict between the two is evidently a source of genuine anguish? Other critics have similarly noted with disapproval how a number of theorists (among them Fredric Jameson and Deleuze and Guattari) see postmodern culture as schizophrenic. They therefore use a traumatic mental disorder in a very casual and clumsy way as a dramatic metaphor to spice up postmodern rhetoric.

Foucault is even more guilty in this respect as he has a tendency to romanticise emotionally disturbed people as subversive elements in society.

It is all very well to sing the praises of irony, playfulness and masquerade in matters of identity, suggests Glass, but what use is that to the client in therapy who does not read postmodern theory? What positive effects can come from denying that their personality has any substance? As well as going against most of our everyday experience, this implies that there is no point in therapy or analysis. Moreover, although many postmodernists do make much of disobedient so-called 'techniques of the body' and 'practices of the self', for Glass it is not easy to reconcile this aspect of their thought with the idea that people are regulated by social codes and structures. In his reading of postmodern theory, people lose most of their free will. Thus postmodernism, despite its apparent aspirations, leaves no space for people to have control over their own lives.

Other critics, more concerned than Glass with preserving a political edge in the face of what they see as postmodernism's lightweight posture of 'anything goes' (see the following chapter for more on this) have remarked on the relative triviality of the 'play, irony and surface' model of subjectivity. To see identity in these terms is a luxury which academics in free and comparatively affluent countries can perhaps afford, but it hardly speaks for the reality of the multiple forms of oppression and misery inflicted on millions of selves the world over.

See: *Shattered Selves: Multiple Personality in a Postmodern World*, by James M. Glass, 1993.

——— The fiction of expression ———

We will now discuss how some of postmodernism's questioning of the self has had repercussions for conventional thinking about artistic creativity and self expression. If the self is decentred, multiple or fractured, and if personal identity can be seen as fundamentally social, as postmodernists insist, what then do we mean when we speak of people expressing themselves? What are the implications for our long established notions of artistic genius and originality?

We are used to thinking about art and other forms of cultural activity in terms of these notions. For example, the belief that the value of Van

Gogh's paintings resides in the way they capture his supposed insanity in oil paint is a clear case of how we habitually associate the meanings of art with the self expression of the geniuses who create it. Similar views are found in popular ideas which circulate about eccentric bohemian artists and temperamental creative types. As well as painters, poets and composers you can find this image of the artistic personality in TV documentaries about fashion designers and rock musicians. Finally the recent fad for releasing restored 'Director's Cut' versions of films, along with the treatment of certain directors as superstars in their own right, shows that although most films are made collectively, we tend to see directors as the ultimate originators and 'explanations' of the films which bear their names.

Especially since the early 1980s there has been an explosion of cultural production which seems to manage without the guiding hand of a genius. Consider the following examples:

- In music we have the common practice of sampling in rap and hip-hop through to various forms of techno. There is also scratching and mixing as a form of musical customisation. The availability of relatively easy to learn digital sequencers and other computerised pieces of musical equipment is making it easier and cheaper for relative beginners to make high-tech records. Many musicians now can hardly be said to be performers in the old sense of the term: making popular music no longer has to depend on virtuoso performances by 'personalities'. (A lot of dance music is now released on 'white label' records by producers and mixers with anonymous-sounding corporate names. These and other factors have to some extent displaced the traditional image of pop stars from the centre of the stage.)

- In architecture, there are signs of a move towards collaborative projects and away (as in music) from the virtuoso performance of the master architect. A well-known example is Ralph Erskine's housing renewal project for the people of Byker in Newcastle, England. Here, locals were encouraged to take part in the design process from the beginning. Far less attention could therefore be paid (as it often had with modernist architecture) to the professional architect using buildings as a platform to show off his own great artistic vision.

- Following the tradition of Andy Warhol's pop art (see Chapter 3), many recent artists have reproduced ready-made objects, images and other works of art. To take two American examples: Sherrie Levine exhibited photographs by famous art photographers and Mike Bidlo did casual renditions of paintings (copied from art books and magazines) by Picasso and others. As with the musical practice of sampling, the use of found materials seems to shift focus away from the importance of originals. When a painter paints a picture of a copy, he has abandoned his conventional role as an observer of forms or a narrator of anguish: there is less opportunity to contemplate his subjective experience. In addition to this there has been a move towards more impersonal media such as video installation. There has also been a widespread willingness among artists to do collaborative pieces and to employ assistants to fabricate their work. So in the art world today there is far less emphasis on the artist's personal touch. Evidence of the individual artist's hand (in brush strokes, say) is much less often elevated to a position of almost mystical importance.

All of these practices have been called postmodern, and this is largely because they are said to subvert modernist ideas about the significance of the individual author in the making of the work. In what follows I will use the term 'author' to refer to any kind of cultural practitioner (e.g. a sculptor, a filmmaker, a choreographer or a poet). I will continue to use the term 'text' in a similarly general way, to signify any artefact produced by an 'author' and exhibited to an audience (e.g. a record, painting, a novel or a film).

—— New romantics, old romantics ——

What is often called the modernist notion of authorship is an extension of romanticism. Romanticism was a loosely defined movement in philosophy and the arts in Europe in the eighteenth and nineteenth centuries. Drawing on the idea that the external world is in some sense a construct of (or at least cannot be separated from) the mind, romanticism exalted the individual self and celebrated the transcendent powers of the imagination. Of course this romantic attitude did not simply die out at some identifiable point in history. As well as carrying on in the modernist art movements, it can still be found in popular ideas that continue to circulate about 'Bohemiam' artists and eccentric geniuses. According to the romantic view, the proper role of art is to reflect the artist's contact with both 'inner' and 'outer' reality. The artist's function is to pierce, participate in, and produce experience. John Ruskin, the nineteenth-century art critic and historian, claimed that the artist must 'go to nature in all singleness of heart, and walk with her laboriously and trustingly, having no thought but how best to penetrate her meaning and remember her instructions . . . rejoicing always in the truth' (note how artists and nature are gendered in this quote). It was seen as the artist's Christian duty to convey to the responsive viewer how the glory of nature (and so of God) was revealed to the artistic imagination. The artist was a gifted being capable of special insights, and the artwork was saturated with this exceptional vision.

In the case of painting, the artist's individual style was often seen as a direct materialisation of the self. As the post-impressionist painter Paul Gauguin put it: 'the work of art for him who can see is a mirror which reflects the artist's soul'. Roger Fry, in his 1909 *Essay in Aesthetics,* similarly observed that the sensations put down in paint by the creators of works of art aroused in the sensitive viewer a profoundly emotional 'special tie with the man who expressed them'. These ideas suppose that the individual artist is a vehicle for truth and authenticity, and that he or she can convey these to the gallery-goer solely through the power of sheer artistic vision. Although the sensitivity of the interpreter of the art work is considered, the meaning of art is basically seen as one-way traffic from the artist, through the artwork and to the reader.

So in the romantic (and common sense) view of authorship it is thought that the meaning found in a text can be readily traced back to its origins in the author. To quote from the French critical theorist Roland Barthes, it is as if 'it were always in the end . . . the voice of a single person, the author, 'confiding' in us'.

Postmodernist critics have attacked the way this romantic approach raises the individual author to unrealistic importance. Some feminist art historians, such as Griselda Pollock, have attacked the macho imagery and male-biased presumptions that often underlie it. You only need to look back at our quotes from Fry and Ruskin to see their point.

Roland Barthes (1925–1980) was one of the figures who helped to formulate a postmodern view of authorship. Associated mainly with structuralism, semiotics and poststructuralism (see Chapter 5), some of Barthes' work set out to question how meaning is produced in works of art. He asked: how are meanings related to their authors? And what is the role of the audience in 'finding' or 'making' these meanings?

─── The Death of the Author ───

In 1968 Barthes published a short essay called *The Death of the Author* in an obscure Parisian literary journal. In 1977, the essay resurfaced in an English translation in a collection of Barthes' essays called *Image – Music – Text* (edited and translated by Stephen Heath). Its original publication in France had caused a few ripples in the world of continental literary theory, but its reappearance a decade later brought it to a much larger audience, and triggered a tidal wave of comment.

It very quickly became something of a canonical piece, widely quoted in books and university courses on critical theory. In the 1980s, it was regularly cited, along with a few other Barthes essays, as an important early statement of the postmodern sensibility, even though Barthes never used the term. The notion of the death of the author also made an impact in the world of art, where it was often cited in relation to the kind of work mentioned above.

Barthes criticises the romantic model on three main counts:

- 'The birth of the reader must be at the cost of the death of the author.'
- 'The text is a tissue of quotations drawn from the innumerable centres of culture.'
- 'It is language which speaks, not the author.'

Each of these phrases is taken from Barthes' essay and each can be read almost as a postmodernist slogan in its own right. So let us give detailed consideration to each in turn.

The birth of the reader must be at the cost of the death of the author

The normal idea of how meaning works assumes that three steps are taken. First, there exists in an individual author an idea, experience, sensation, or mental state. This occurs in the author independently of any verbal or visual language. It does not signify anything yet. It just is. This is close to what we mean by the moment of inspiration. Second, the author shapes inspiration into meaning by manipulating a particular medium. In other words, his or her inspiration is put into signs (words, images, etc.) Third, these signs convey the meaning given by the author and an audience is able to read them. The meaning as it occurred in the author can be read off the signs.

This model of meaning assumes that the author occupies the centre of the work and is the dominant source of meaning. The text is simply a vessel for meanings which are poured into it by the author. Language therefore simply carries meaning. The role of the reader as an interpreter of the text is essentially to receive meaning and not to create it.

But Barthes reminds us that any text can exist in any number of different times and places unforeseen when the author originally conceived it. A text moves through history, geography and culture, constantly gathering new meanings and revising old ones as it goes. There is no reason to assume that a Shakespeare play means exactly the same thing today as it did when first performed, for example. Yet when critics focus on the image of the 'genius' who produced the work, they try to restrict the changeable nature of meaning: they attempt to make the meanings of the text seem more timeless and stable than they really are.

Elsewhere in his essay Barthes notes that 'a text's unity lies not in its origin, but in its destination'. A text is only a random mass of signs until a reader comes along and binds them together in a way which lends them coherence. The most common way of binding them together, as we have seen, is in the shape of the author. But there is no reason to suppose that there even *should* be anything coherent about a text. By ignoring what Barthes calls the 'tyrannical' notion of genius, you give the signs more freedom to play, and you liberate the reader to invent new meanings. So the 'destination' of a text is its moment of being read. Of course, there can never be only one such destination, and the author has a very limited amount of control (if any) over where the text goes and what people do with it.

The text is a tissue of quotations drawn from the innumerable centres of culture

In his book *The Archaeology of Knowledge* (1969, first published in English in 1972), Michel Foucault wrote that:

❝ the frontiers of a book are never clear-cut: beyond the title, the first line and the last full stop, beyond its internal configuration... it is caught up in a system of references to other books, other texts, other sentences . . . The book is not simply the object that one holds in one's hands . . . its unity is variable and relative. **❞**

(page 23)

Borrowing the word from another of his contemporaries, Julia Kristeva (see Chapter 5), Barthes called the condition of texts described by Foucault *intertextuality*. One way of understanding this term is as a sort of environment of texts in which an author works and from which she or he draws. Whatever original idea an author might have, certain conditions must be in place in order for these ideas to 'happen'. An important aspect of these conditions is the fact that his or her text, and even the desire to produce it, exists inescapably in relation to a vast number of other texts, mostly by other authors. So no text sits in a vacuum or speaks its own tongue. Authors have to get their ideas from somewhere, and readers can only read in the light of what they have seen before.

Certain artefacts are very noticeably intertextual. That is to say, they overtly refer to other texts. Many spoof films like *Hot Shots* or *Spy Hard*, for example, are intertextual in the sense that they obviously make all sorts of references to other films (*Rambo*, *Pulp Fiction*, *Die Hard* and *Apocalypse Now*, among many others, have all been parodied in these films). Modernist novels like James Joyce's *Ulysses* (1922) also self-consciously refer to other writings. In *Ulysses* Joyce re-worked the themes of Homer's *Odyssey* and played with all sorts of styles, from Chaucer to modern day beauty-advice columns.

Intertextuality: a postmodern style?

Some critics have found the idea of intertextuality to be a good descriptions, a peculiarly contemporary aesthetic. We can all think of recent records which have mixed references to music from many different times and places, for example. Fashion design, too, is enormously wide-ranging in the way it can take ideas from any point in the entire history and geography of dress. And if you like to put your eclectic book, video and souvenir collections on display, then maybe even your shelves can be seen in a similar way. Since all of these might be said to 'draw from the innumerable centres of culture' they might all be seen as intertextual art forms. In this understanding of the term, intertextuality is a style intensified (and perhaps created) by the increasingly pluralistic, cosmopolitan nature of postmodern society.

Jean Baudrillard's take on such postmodern intertextuality (see Chapter 4 for more on him) is not so enthusiastic. Redefining intertextuality as a 'single dimension' of 'promiscuous' sounds and images, he notes that the whole world now appears to unfold on our televisions and radios as a haphazard mixture of contradictory information. Postmodern intertextuality for Baudrillard means being swamped by a 'pornography of information . . . a pornography of all functions and objects in their readability, their fluidity, their availability'. The problem is that in this process everything becomes equal and in doing so loses its true sense of meaning and reality.

But in fact *all* texts are intertextual. In all acts of authorship, no matter how small, we draw from a vast repertoire of codes, conventions and influences. If I were to carve a pair of initials and a love heart into the bark of a tree, for example, that act would have been informed by all the love hearts on trees I have seen represented before. And *those* representations would themselves echo countless other ways of picturing affection. And so on, down an infinite chain of influences and references.

Thus intertextuality is not so much a matter of style as a structural property which allows readers to read and texts to be produced. A text only gathers meaning because it is, as Barthes says, 'woven entirely with citations, references, echoes, cultural languages'. It is both inscribed with the traces of the texts that have gone before it, and formed in the act of reading by the encyclopaedia of references we all carry with us as participants in culture.

The reading of a text is always allowed by knowledges and expectations produced in our 'intertextual landscape'. In her *The Scorsese Connection* (1995) the film critic Lesley Stern has taken these principles on board by writing a book, apparently on the American director Martin Scorsese, which spends more time teasing out strange echoes of other films than it does on explaining Scorsese's own work. One chapter alone drifts in and out of all sorts of odd connections between Jerry Lewis movies, *Blue Velvet*, *The Wizard of Oz*, horror films, the New York underground cinema, the B-movie director Roger Corman, and Alfred Hitchcock. Somewhere in there are a couple of Scorsese films, but these are never presented as in any way 'central'. Rather than simply being unique pieces of art springing from the head of a unique film artist, Scorsese's movies are treated as part of a vast inter-textual field which no individual film maker can dominate. All films resonate with one another's images and meanings. As Barthes would put it, a film 'is but a space in which a variety of images, none of them original, blend and clash'. So it makes no sense to try and explain Scorsese in terms of his own talent, life story or intentions. Because you can only watch films through the rest of their cultural surround-ings Sterne's book is not so much about Scorsese as *around* him.

It is language which speaks, not the author

This third phrase is perhaps the most radical claim in Barthes' essay. What Barthes is arguing against here is the taken-for-granted view that ideas spontaneously occur in the mind of the author, as if from nowhere, and are secondarily put into words or other signs. This con-ventional view suggests that there is a pure realm of ideas which exists prior to language, and that we can simply freely choose the best signs with which to express those ideas.

From Barthes' perspective, there are a couple of major theoretical problems here:

● You cannot have an idea without it *already* arriving to you in the form of signs. You cannot have a language-less thought. Your ideas are restricted to what your language has made available to you.

● Language is therefore active: it speaks. Signs produce, rather than passively mirror, meaning.

For example: a Monet painting does not innocently capture the fleet-ing effects of sunlight on a boating-lake. We have simply learned to read the signs in such a way that they produce (rather than reflect) that image for us. A very different example: the clothes and behaviour of a person do not express individuality, they make it. The notion of expression suggests that meaning (in this case, individuality) is simply *there*, waiting for the appropriate signs (in this case fashion and body language) to come along and embody it. But there is not an 'individual identity' until certain clothes and behaviour have been adopted. Their expressive qualities are not invented out of the blue. They work because our culture has encoded them in certain ways. In a sense it is the whole of culture, not the 'author', which is speaking. Thus meaning does not travel *from* a vacuum *to* a sign. The sign *is* the meaning.

—————————— Summary ——————————

Authorship is (or should be) dead because:

- the author is not available for study; what we usually have before us is not an author, but a text

- no author can control the various interpretations that people will give to his or her work

- words generate meanings free of the author's wishes, and authors cannot 'master' language in its entirety

- what the author puts into the text is the product of language and culture more than of personal intention

- the only point of the idea of genius is to mystify art; examining the self expression of authors distracts from art's social and political aspects.

Postmodernists do not deny that there are people in the world who have intentions when they write, paint, make movies or whatever. They just ask us to reconsider the faith we place in them.

Criticisms

Ideas of authorship are still worth having because:

- Without the author you imply that a text is 'just' a text. In other words, you imply that it is just a free-floating combination of words and images. So despite some of the above claims, the 'death of the author' can be viewed as excessively antihistorical and asocial.

- Reminding yourself of who authored a text can usefully restore it to the circumstances in which it was originally made. You cannot have a proper understanding of a text without knowing something about the 'who, where and when' of it. Texts are made by real people in concrete situations, so looking at the author is a useful way into these questions.

- Doing away with the figure of the author erases the significance of identity politics. It negates important questions concerning what social and cultural identities are being given a voice in the text. Surely it is significant, for example, whether the author is white or black, male or female, gay or straight, but the 'death of the author' wipes these matters away.

- Authors can often provide important models for people to identify with or aspire to.

- If intentions are irrelevant, if meaning is uncontrollable, we might as well give up on trying to say anything.

And a final note of caution

Barthes' essay is nearly always understood to be a general reflection on all forms of authorship and all forms of author. But an alternative reading is possible which suggests that the essay really offers a veiled form of elitism. In this interpretation, the author Barthes is so keen to assassinate is only the author of conventional realistic novels. Barthes can be seen as arguing for very particular sorts of 'difficult' writing, and for the writers of these works. Thus the 'birth of the reader' is not a spontaneous consumer revolution or a simple shift in what literary critics should attend to. Instead it is the outcome of experimental literature (Barthes would praise Brecht, Joyce, Mallarmé, Surrealism, etc.) which supposedly acts to make reading a more creative process than people normally undergo in their consumption of 'low culture'.

Conclusion

As we have seen, there are many aspects to the theorisation of postmodern identity, but central is the idea of the *fundamentally social self*. Postmodern thoery may not have the monopoly on this basic notion, but it does elaborate on it in its own particular ways. In Jean Baudrillard's terms, for example (see chapter 4), simulation has imploded into private life to such an extent that it has become impossible to distinguish between 'natural' and 'manufactured' identities and desires. Some critics have responded by seeking a more positive view of how senses of identity can be created through the consumption of mass-produced objects and images. For Barthes and others the out-come has been a reconsideration of the idea of artistic 'self-expression'.

Key questions asked of the self by postmodernism include:

- Where are the boundaries of the self?
- Is it possible to distinguish in any clear way between private/public or inner/outer selves?
- Has the time come for the image of the whole, unified and profound self to be replaced by a multiple, fractured and superficial model?

How do we learn to handle the fact that we may already be little more than *Bladerunner*-like replicants? What can we do with the fact that identity seems to be becoming ever more fragmentary and unstable? Of course there are no ready answers to these questions. The post-modernised self is in many ways still in the process of being defined. Theoretical accounts of it have largely remained (like the vision of the self they describe) partial and fragmentary. Foucault suggested that 'modern man' may be becoming extinct, but perhaps it is too early as yet to know how we are going to live with 'his' death.

8

THEORISING THE
BROKEN WORLD

A number of key ideas about postmodernism have been dealt with in different ways throughout this book. We can summarise these ideas as the following very crude set of 'fors' and 'againsts':

Postmodernism is *against*:

- ideas about depth and essence
- the total and universal.

Postmodernism is *for*:

- the superficial and provisional
- fragmentation and difference.

In this final chapter we will draw out and further explore postmodernism's treatment of the last of these points. But before we get into the details a few general observations will provide useful background.

Politicians often use the idea of 'we the people' in their speeches to conjure up an image of community and national identity. When they use this phrase they effectively suggest that we are all on 'the same team'. But many postmodern theorists argue to the contrary. They suggest that society is in an important sense incoherent and that no single perspective can grasp the complexity and fluidity of current conditions. They say that society has fragmented into so many conflicting knowledges, identities, needs and views that it is neither possible nor desirable to see the human race as one big family.

This situation arises partly out of the fact that our societies are becoming increasingly multi-cultural and our lifestyles are becoming more and more cosmopolitan. But it can also be taken to mean that (a) there is no agreement about what is worth believing (or even knowing) any more, (b) that social conditions are in a frightening state of disrepair, or (c) a combination of the two. Some postmodernists think that it is pointless to complain about this state of affairs. They see it as far more constructive to push the fragmentation as far as it will go and use it to your advantage.

When politicians and others use the word 'we' they are often trying to smooth out or disguise the presence of disagreement and diversity. Many postmodernists prefer to take the opposite approach. They propose that we should activate the differences between people and between the cultural spaces they inhabit; this is the only way to generate new ideas and experiences. As well as possibilities for creativity, this obviously contains the potential for violent conflict, but it seems that some postmodern thinkers would rather see violence than flabby tolerance.

We can begin to explore these points by concentrating on one of the most influential texts of postmodern theory, *The Postmodern Condition* by Jean-Francois Lyotard (1924–). Although Lyotard's focus in that work is mainly on science, we will go on to see how some of the topics he addresses have had repercussions for the study of culture at large.

—— Lyotard: when worlds collide ——

The Postmodern Condition was first published in 1979 as a report, commissioned by Quebec's Conseil des Universités, on the state of scientific knowledge and information in the late twentieth century. Lyotard's central concern is the grounds of knowledge. He is interested in how forms of knowledge come into being, who controls and has access to them, and how they become accepted as valid. His basic argument is that because of broad changes in culture and society scientific disciplines no longer assume that their theories and discoveries have universal or timeless value.

The truth is not out there

Thanks to commercials which use 'lab technicians' as a source of evidence about the germ-killing capacities of particular brands of bleach, or which stress the clinically proven ability of a certain sort of toothpaste to fight plaque, we are used to thinking of scientists as holders of truth. When we speak of evidence as scientific, we tend to mean that it is neutral and that it is therefore closer to reality than mere opinion. TV news and documentary programmes often make use of the fact that as soon as we are shown a man in a white coat discussing his latest discovery in a lab or book-lined study, we assume that he knows what he is talking about. We might also believe that his research is conducted in an objective spirit of scientific enquiry, that his discoveries add to our ever-growing knowledge about the universe, and that if science has a goal it is to improve the lot of humanity.

Lyotard builds his analysis of the current state of scientific knowledge around the assertion that these kinds of ideas are outmoded myths. He argues that theory is never neutral, and follows thinkers like Michel Foucault and Jacques Derrida in looking at how knowledge is always limited by the institutions in which it is created (see Chapter 5 for more on this). From this perspective, scientists can have no more direct access to 'the truth' than can philosophers or historians. For Lyotard, they are all story-tellers, and the narratives they produce (e.g. research papers, hypotheses, histories) are always governed by the protocols of the field in which they work. Each discipline is like a game: it has a special language which only makes sense within its own boundaries. Rather than being faced with infinite possibilities, a theorist or researcher can only play within the limits of a system of permissible moves.

So science is made up of language games which generate particular forms of narrative. Clearly this goes against the common sense view of science as a superior form of knowledge. It also contradicts modern science's view of itself. In order to maintain its high status, science has often tried to deny its own involvement in story-telling. It pretends to be beyond narrative. How does science do this? Ironically enough, it does it by appealing to what Lyotard calls grand *metanarratives*.

A *metanarrative* is an over-arching story which can supposedly account for, explain, or comment upon the validity of all other stories, a universal or absolute set of truths which is supposed to transcend social, institutional or human limitations.

For example, a small, local narrative or language game (e.g. the result of a scientific experiment, an individual's life story) is usually granted significance only by its ability to reflect or support 'global' narratives like those of progress, truth and justice.

From big science to little sciences

Lyotard assumes that in earlier modern times (around the eighteenth century onwards) faith was placed in science as the source of enlightenment. For instance, instead of answering to religion as the guarantee of truth, political and economic fields developed which claimed to have the standing of science. Being 'scientific' or 'rational' was now a sign of credibility. Possessing scientific knowledge implied that you could get behind mystification and superstition, reveal the facts about the world and lead all of humanity to a brighter day.

Condensed in this view are a number of important assumptions about science:

- It is progressive, moving towards a state of 'complete knowledge'.

- It is unified; there may be many different areas within science, but deep down they all share the same goal.

- It is universal – science works for the good of all of us, and aims at total truths which will benefit all of human life.

Between the enlightenment age and the mid-twentieth century, science justified itself by claiming that it needed no justification. That is to say, it took advantage of the idea that its activities were pursued in the name of the timeless metanarratives of progress, emancipation, and knowledge. By appealing in this way to ideas whose meanings are taken to be self-evident and universally agreed, science was able to masquerade as a single project objectively carried out for the good of the 'human race'.

Lyotard claims that since around the end of the Second World War, these myths have collapsed. Some of the reasons for this collapse are outlined below:

Science's contribution to ecological disaster, and the development of nuclear and chemical weapons, has made it difficult to link scientific rationality with 'progress'. Partly as a result of this there is now widespread suspicion towards big enlightenment stories. Lyotard therefore defines postmodernism as an attitude of 'incredulity towards metanarratives'.

Explorations in the philosophy and sociology of science have recognised the influence on science of social processes, and have questioned the idea of 'objectivity' (of particular influence was Thomas Kuhn: *The Structure of Scientific Revolutions'* (1960).

Approaches like 'chaos theory', quantum mechanics, etc. have highlighted uncertainty in measurement. Because of these influences it has become harder to see science as the activity of a rational mind confronting a concrete reality.

The spirit of commercial free enterprise has entered research and has contributed to the rapid growth of computerised means of information processing. The outcome of this has been that theories and discoveries are now judged on the basis of performance and efficiency rather then truth or purpose. Scientists are now primarily interested in putting out work which will both generate further research funding and add to their own power and prestige within the academic 'market place'.

Once, ideas developed within 'natural philosophy' were bound together through theology. No hard and fast boundaries divided philosophy from science, or what we now call 'physics' from what is now known as 'chemistry'. Knowledge had not yet reached the stage where it was necessary to create these separate disciplines, and where it was a lifetime's work to master just one of them. It was possible to be a Renaissance person, capable of holding on to a thorough knowledge of many different aspects of natural philosophy. Now, rather than being a single endeavour travelling in a single direction towards a single goal, science has splintered into a mass of specialisms. In place of centralised metanarratives which bind all of these specialisms together, we now have a multitude of disciplines and sub-disciplines which all follow their own agendas and speak their own languages. According to Lyotard, sciences today are therefore more sceptical about the possibility of penetrating *the* truth or finding *the* answer.

So sciences are now carried out on a more modest, limited level. Realising that they cannot find permanent answers to everything, they only come up with temporarily valid opinions, and seek to solve merely immediate, local problems.

So postmodern science:

- is not coherent
- can no longer be valued for the contribution it makes towards human progress
- has abandoned the idea that one day the sum of all knowledge will add up to a state of perfect information
- has become a mass of incompatible little sciences with no goal other than to generate further research.

The splintering of knowledge discussed by Lyotard is paralleled by a wider sense of social and cultural disintegration. Thus his report has found many echoes in fields as diverse as political theory, cultural theory and art criticism. Indeed, later editions of the book include a postscript which concentrates on aesthetic rather than scientific issues, and the text as a whole can be read as an overview of how the 'rules of the game' have apparently changed in culture at large. It is perhaps not surprising to learn, therefore, that 'the postmodern condition' has had more of an impact on the humanities than it has had on the 'hard' sciences. In order to gauge some of this impact, we will now look at how the issues addressed by Lyotard have had repercussions for political and social thought.

— The transformation of Marxism —

Political thought under the influence of Marx has tended to see social class as the key site of oppression, and the resulting conflict between dominant and subordinate classes as the basis for future revolution. In this view faith is put in the proletariat as the universal class which will lead the way to socialism, and the economic structure is seen as the determining factor in social and cultural life. But much postmodern thought has challenged the idea that any one class, structure or factor can single-handedly explain history or bring about change. Following many of the themes we have touched on with Lyotard, Foucault, Baudrillard and others, this post-Marxist tendency seeks a less reductive view of history and society, and tries to formulate a more radical version of democracy than Marxism has often provided. It aims to address political theory to a more chaotic social landscape full of fluid identities and diverse social groups. It asks whether revolution is still possible in an age apparently without agreed values, and whether radical gestures can have any effect in a world which seems able to absorb all attempts at subversion.

There are two main aspects to this shift:

A new map of power

Since the late 1980s the collapse of communism and the apparent end of the cold war between what were once the two world superpowers have re-drawn the political map of the world. This has been echoed in some countries by a gradual meeting in the middle of the main left and right political parties (e.g. the rhetoric of the Democrats and the Republicans in America, and Labour and Conservative in Britain becoming increasingly similar).

Class fragmentation

Political and social identity cannot be reduced to a unified picture of an economically based class system. Gender, ethnic identity, age, sexual orientation and so on all cut across and fracture the image of class. There has also been a shift in industrial production from the standardisation to the diversification of output (a move away from Henry Ford's ideas about mass production). This has resulted, among other things, in the intensification of niche marketing whereby ever more particular taste-groups are identified and 'exploited'.

Partly because of these influences reasonably affluent members of contemporary capitalist societies are more able to experiment with tastes, images and lifestyles than ever before, and as a result they are now much less likely to identify with their class origins.

The cultural politics of how minority groups are represented in the media now seems to have a louder voice than politics drawn along the traditional lines of conflict between the bourgeoisie and the proletariat. Wrangles over the right of people to express their own sexual and cultural identities have increased in prominence. Issues as diverse as the rights of the disabled, nuclear and environmental protest and animal rights have also become increasingly hot news. In India recently, members of women's groups threatened to set fire to themselves in protest at the 1996 Miss World contest. In America, elections have been fought on the basis of debates about abortion. In Britain, white members of parliament have involved themselves in arguments about the lyrics of some black American rap records. Heated exchanges have taken place on TV about everything from the rights and wrongs of Michael Jackson making himself look Caucasian to the 'problem' of showing lesbian kisses on prime time soap operas. These various struggles are all examples of cultural and identity politics. All of them (and of course there are many more) have seemed to push class war away from the heart of political activism. People are now more concerned with fighting over specific individual issues than they are with large-scale party politics. Public participation in elections shrinks every year, yet the number of issues available to be fought over seems to grow daily as the true diversity of human life comes increasingly into the light. The shift towards this 'grass roots level' politics is further discussed below.

In short, postmodernism erodes the three touchstones of modern politics:

- nation
- class
- belief in the wholesale transformation of the world.

Postmodern micropolitics

As Lyotard argues, there is no great blueprint which binds all 'language games' together. There is no reason to believe that different pieces of knowledge share conceptual ground or that, at the end of the day, they all contribute to one vast human enterprise. Preferring the image of chaos to that of progress, Lyotard pictures a world in which all the grand ideas collapse, and no idea assumes more than a partial value. Truth is a short-term contract here. You cannot speak in the name of universal human principles and expect them to form a fixed standard by which to judge other people's perspectives. You can no longer look to ideas like morality, justice, enlightenment or human nature and expect them to form a globally agreed basis for your own point of view. It is impossible to draw up a complete map of the world in such a way that everybody would be able to recognise it as representing their own knowledge and experience. Postmodernists argue that it is no longer possible to write a 'theory of everything'.

Micropolitics

Many theorists of postmodern society argue that power no longer works by a single monolithic state or class inflicting itself on the masses. People are not simply oppressed and exploited from above. Rather, power is exerted through the apparently mundane little networks of everyday life. Everything from advertising and other forms of representation through to interpersonal relationships and shopping can now be seen as caught up in multiple systems of power. To this extent much postmodern theory assumes that everything is in some sense political. On the one hand this means that just about anything is capable of being 'oppressive'. On the other hand it suggests that you can just as easily find acts of resistance to that oppression in the most seemingly trivial of places.

Thus postmodernism has a more modest notion of what counts as political action. Rather than aiming your beliefs at some grand Utopian scheme which will transform human destiny, postmodern politics suggests that it is more worthwhile to challenge power on a day-to-day level. Thus postmodern politics looks for ways in which we can all, as Lyotard puts it, 'gnaw away at the great institutionalised narrative apparatuses . . . by increasing the number of skirmishes that take place on the sidelines. That's what women who have had abortions, prisoners, conscripts, prostitutes, students, and peasants have been doing . . .' And, it is argued, that is what we can all do.

Rather than having to enrol in the project of total human emancipation, we are just as politically engaged every time we have a quarrel with a racist neighbour, refuse to buy a certain brand of condensed milk, or borrow our office's fax machine for personal correspondence. Everything from defacing billboards to selling pirate copies of banned video tapes can now be seen as an attempt to gnaw away at the powers-that-be. None of these activities might strike you as particularly radical – they are perhaps not going to bring about a revolution – but from Lyotard's point of view they can be valued as disruptive skirmishes in the social system.

Lyotard's celebration of small-scale acts of dissent and his view of political commitment as a matter of personal games and tactics can be seen as part of a libertarian strand within postmodern theory: he places individual freedom at the centre of his philosophy. We already encountered something of this tendency with Foucault, Derrida and others, all of whom expressed mistrust of any kind of totalising or centralising thought or action. Although there are differences between these thinkers, all have regarded 'universalising' enlightenment theories (of history, progress, knowledge and so on) as more or less authoritarian ways of trying to produce conformity.

Other key books by Lyotard include:

Libidinal Economy (1974, English translation 1993)
The Differend: Phrases in Dispute (1983, English translation 1986).

The techniques of daily life

This postmodern or post-Marxist view of political action as something which can take place on the most commonplace and normally overlooked of levels is influenced by a book by Michel de Certeau called *The Practice of Everyday Life* (first English translation 1989). De Certeau argues that in order to understand the present way of life you should attend less to an overall picture of society as a whole and more to the seemingly insignificant details of how people go about living their lives. By doing so you will find in contemporary life not some falsely unified spirit of the age, but a complex mass of interweaving and contradictory desires, concerns and stories.

For de Certeau everyday life is creative. When we go shopping we are drawing our own conceptual maps through the city streets. When we zap across the channels on our TV sets we are creating moving collages from materials provided by the mass media. When we buy fake designer labels, we are undermining the elitist fashion system. And when we tape music from the radio we are subversively stealing from the owners of the airwaves. According to de Certeau everyday life is full of such acts of 'poaching, tricking, speaking, strolling, desiring'.

Hence he refuses to see us as the passive victims of consumer society. Rather than simply swallowing the goods, environments and lifestyles imposed on us by an all-powerful capitalist system, we employ all sorts of techniques to make our material conditions bearable and to make sense of the world we live in. Every day we engage in the creative production of our own power struggles, pleasures and acts of disobedience, and in doing so we create important cracks in the monolith of 'the dominant economic order'. We may not be able to change the world, de Certeau suggests, but at least we can migrate across the cultural environment, taking bits we need from whatever products and experiences are available. In short, day-to-day life is about making do against the system.

Conclusion

- Postmodernist theory is sceptical of any totalising attempt to achieve global harmony through the wholesale application of universal ideals.

- It drops the dream of a future Utopia in favour of a politics of the here and now.

- Its view of what counts as radical instead embraces temporary acts of resistance within the limits of regional conditions and demands. (This can be compared to similar moves within postmodernist architecture – see the section on Robert Venturi in Chapter 2 of this book.)

- It celebrates a world in which principles are constantly in the process of being fought over and redefined. It sees no reason to hope that this process will some day come to an end.

—— Criticisms of post-Marxism ——

A number of thinkers who place themselves politically on the left have had their doubts about the claims outlined above. They see in the theories of Lyotard, de Certeau and the rest a sell-out of genuinely radical political ideas, and find in their place a lazy acceptance of the way things are. From this point of view postmodernism is, despite its radical sounding terminology, a deeply conservative response to the ideals promoted by modernity. Its theories are too close for comfort to the ideas they pretend to oppose:

- Its celebration of fragmentation and difference in society seems to strike at the heart of socialism's fundamental faith in community and collective action. It complies too happily with the idea of the 'free market'.

- Its rejection of the idea of progress implies that there is no point in anyone trying to make the world a better place.

- Its fascination with commodities, fashion and the media shows that it is so seduced by capitalism that it has lost its critical distance.

- Its interest in how consumers make the best of a bad situation seems far too laid back and defeatist.

- Its emphasis on the 'politics of identity' is a poor substitute for genuine 'hard' political activity.

One of the key figures in the critical response towards postmodern theory is Jurgen Habermas.

Habermas takes on postmodernism

Habermas (1929–) continues the enquiries of the Frankfurt School of critical theory, whose work we have come across elsewhere in this book (see Chapter 6 for example). He shares with them, and also with many postmodernists, a general uneasiness towards rational systems, and agrees with them that the technical rationality of science should be treated with suspicion. Like Lyotard and others, Habermas believes that the products of modernity (technology, science, capitalist economic systems, etc.) have so far failed to live up to their potential. They have tended to enslave people rather than liberate them, and instead of enriching creativity they have often impoverished it. However, Habermas sees postmodern thought as 'the end of the Enlightenment', and goes against Lyotard by believing that the project of modernity is still worth pursuing.

Although he is very wary of present political and economic systems (whether capitalist or communist) which regulate people's lives, Habermas is no anarchist. He sees postmodernism's apparent embrace of irrationality as morally bankrupt and believes, contrary to Lyotard, that some sort of universally agreed-upon framework is both possible and necessary in order to ensure that freedom and justice are achieved. We can move towards this goal by bringing the spheres of morality, science and art back together, removing them from the experts and professionals who currently monopolise them, and restoring them to ordinary people. Habermas disputes the claims of some postmodern thinkers that human identity is unstable, fragmented, or 'in process' (see Chapter 6 for more on this): for him we all, deep down, share eternal human needs and desires. The failure of the postmodernists is that they refuse to propose a route towards the fulfilment of these.

Lyotard argued that it is impossible to create any single ethical scheme which does not silence or alienate minority voices, but Habermas responds that as long as we can freely communicate with each other we will one day all agree about what the true values are and how to make them happen. Disputing the postmodernist's claim that all moral concepts are open to different interpretations, he asks: 'How is it possible to follow a moral programme if you do not believe it to be universally right?' Unless we believe that the great ideals of freedom, justice and democracy can be fully realised, we will never be able to progress towards the global emancipation of humanity. Through the process of open and rational conversation we need to keep searching for the common ethical ground which lies beneath our superficial differences.

So Lyotard is mistaken in his belief that the Enlightenment project is exhausted. This attitude is conservative in that, seeing principles as nothing more than language games, it opens the way to the casual acceptance of any and every aberrant point of view. For Habermas, unlike Lyotard, it is not modernity's ideas of enlightenment, reason and rationality that are wrong, so much as the misuse to which history has sometimes put them. Mistakes may often have been made in the name of modernity but we still need to hold on to at least some of its aspirations. By opening up knowledge and the means of communication to people it is possible to enhance their understanding of themselves and others, and in doing so to promote progress towards human happiness. Thus the promise of the modern 'project' needs to be completed rather than abandoned.

One of Habermas' key books is *The Philosophical Discourse of Modernity* (1995). His most well known essay is 'Modernity: An Incomplete Project'. This can be found in *Postmodernism; a Reader*, edited by Thomas Docherty (1993).

Lyotard's defence

It can seem that Lyotard's kind of postmodernism involves a complete rejection of morality. And it is true to say that the trend has been for promoting the pursuit of pleasure over moral responsibility. But Lyotard's anarchic abandonment of 'universal' ideals is motivated largely by an idealistic desire to maximise freedom and creativity. Out of this desire he has expressed concern with the control of knowledge in our society, and has argued that in order to shift power back from systems to individuals the public should be granted free access to all information. So Lyotard does have quite firm ethics. He just does not believe they can ever apply to all people for all time. The difficulty then is how to persuade people that your values are correct without at the same time appearing authoritarian or violent (by trying to silence 'marginal' voices).

Lyotard has compared speaking to fighting and claims that what we should aim for is not so much the satisfaction of winning as the pleasures of keeping up the fight. Difference is always more desirable than agreement, for it is from difference that invention arises. The lines should always be kept open: universal agreement about values should be discouraged rather than encouraged, because consensus – if such a thing is even possible – only 'does violence to the heterogeneity of language games', as Lyotard says. So the fear among postmodernists is that universal principles threaten cultural diversity by seeking to force a single way of life on people. As far as Lyotard is concerned the only way to avoid such terroristic suppression of different experiences, identities, and expressions is to forget the prospect of unity and to dismantle any institution which aims at 'governing the social bonds':

> ❻ The idea that I think we need today in order to make decisions in political matters cannot be the idea of the totality, or of the unity, of the body. It can only be the idea of a mutiplicity or of a diversity. ❾
>
> Steven Best & Douglas Kellner, *Postmodern Theory: Critical Interrogations* (1991) page 89

Conclusion

Postmodern or post-Marxist politics gives critics a range of problems. It can be argued that while the postmodern approach is constructive in its search for new possibilities for political radicalism, it easily slips into a far too passive 'anything goes' attitude. So the strength of the kind of angles discussed above lies in their desire to support all forms of cultural and individual diversity. But their weakness lies in the fact that this desire can often result in an enfeebling form of relativism. For example, one result of this in the area of cultural studies is that many researchers now want to celebrate rather than criticise popular culture. To exercise your critical skills on the little politics of identity and consumption is to allow yourself the luxury of being distracted from the real problems of poverty and injustice that still beset this supposedly late capitalist society. What use, after all, is a theory of mass consumption to people forced to live on the streets? Hence the British critic Simon Frith has argued that too many analysts of culture have left political engagement behind in favour of the sound of the cash register. Another British critic, Colin MacCabe, has similarly suggested recently that postmodernism has encouraged too much cultural 'pick and mix' and not enough hard thinking. The time has come, he says, for theorists to reject all this disabling pluralism and learn how to make value judgements again.

Postmodern space

Thanks in part to this interest in miniature tactics of political resistance – what Michel Foucault (see Chapter 7) called 'the little tactics of the habitat' – recent thinking about postmodernism has taken a particular interest in space and location. Let us look at some examples.

Edward Soja

An American geographer, Soja has argued that we tend to see history (or time) as the major force behind culture and society, as though it travels under its own steam, influencing people and places as it moves along. Once again it is Marxism which Soja wants to give a facelift in this respect. He claims that traditional Marxism places too much weight on the idea of the progress of history towards a single goal. This view shunts geography too far into the background, making it the canvas on which history paints itself. In other words, space is seen as something which is merely acted on by time. Soja sees this model as too simplistic and aims to go beyond it by putting space into the foreground. Pointing out that we live in concrete environments as much as we live in abstract constructs like society and time, he argues that spaces actively affect history rather than passively receive it.

Soja asserts that it is pointless for thinkers with radical political aspirations to simply wish postmodernism away. Postmodernism is not an attitude you can choose to approve or disapprove of. It is a set of concrete conditions which now affect all aspects of contemporary life, and they will continue to do so whether you like it or not. He believes that the future of radical politics depends on its ability to come to terms with these conditions.

Over the last few decades a postmodern reorganisation of space has emerged which has begun to radically alter both the way we live and the way we see the world. He looks in particular at the postmodern city (which he calls the 'post-metropolis'), and observes there a mixture of transformations in the arrangement of urban places. Cities have been undergoing many complex processes of postmodernisation which have affected what Soja sees as 'urbanised' ways of living and thinking. Among the (sometimes contradictory) restructurings noted by Soja are:

Drastic changes in industry

These include the computerised design and production of goods alongside craft-based industries, the growth of industries (e.g. the stock exchange, financial advisors) based on selling information, a widening of the gap between rich and poor (often living in close proximity to each other) and a weakening of trade union power.

The growth of global cities

Soja cites the ways in which multinational corporations spread their offices, outlets, advertising campaigns, logos and factories all over the world, the Internet continues to grow, there is an increase in 'global identities' as more and more people seek work away from their home countries, and there is an international division of labour between 'First', 'Second' and 'Third' worlds.

Increasing surveillance

Soja points out that communities and individuals are becoming more and more obsessed with security, and notes that in the USA at least

30,000 communities are literally fenced off to keep intruders at bay. Crime prevention is now an industry in its own right. Ever increasing numbers of city streets are being installed with surveillance cameras. Numerous identity card schemes and neighbourhood watch schemes are introduced. The postmodernised space is a site of prohibition and supervision.

Soja's key work is *Postmodern Geographies: The Reassertion of Space in Critical Social Theory*, 1989.

Fredric Jameson

We have noted elsewhere in this book that Jameson, although partly excited by the dynamic and witty quality of some postmodern culture, is worried about what he sees as its superficiality. From architecture and literature through to music videos and cinema, too much of today's culture, he suggests in his book *Postmodernism, or the Cultural Logic of Late Capitalism*, is made up of hollow signs thrown together in meaningless combinations. Jameson sees everywhere a general 'waning of affect' and defines this as a loss of historical awareness which makes everything seem equally lightweight. We now live in a dangerously short-sighted 'perpetual present' in which society has lost its ability to know its own past. Profound meanings and deep interpretations have been replaced by surfaces which play among themselves in the centreless space of global media.

For Jameson this postmodern culture of surfaces is intimately related to certain technological, economic and political changes. Borrowing themes from a number of theorists of what has been called 'post-industrial' society (especially Daniel Bell and Ernest Mandel), he proposes that postmodernism is the 'cultural logic' of our current stage of capitalist expansion and implies that everything produced within it is postmodern in character. Although the transition to this logic cannot reliably be dated to a single point in time, Jameson puts forward the following broad shifts:

Market capitalism

Associated with the eighteenth and nineteenth centuries, this phase was based on industrial growth within individual nations. It was characterised by the rise of the 'self-made man' (the factory owner, the 'fat cat' capitalist).

Monopoly capitalism

Associated with the mid-nineteenth to mid-twentieth centuries, this is the so-called imperialist phase in which capitalism profited from the creation of more and more foreign markets for the production and consumption of goods. Colonised nations (e.g. those in the 'third world') were exploited for cheap labour and raw materials.

Multinational capitalism

Also known as 'consumer', 'late' or 'post-industrial' capitalism, this is the current state of affairs in which we witness the growth of an international market in images and information. Jameson paints this phase as a world of global telecommunication networks and huge media webs spanning continents. Here representations and data become commodities circulated electronically in virtual superhighways. Information networks run over national boundaries, and a vast network of multinational business corporations holds more power than individual nation states.

At the same time, capitalist expansion has created ever smaller groups of consumers – with specialised tastes and interests – for their ever-growing range of different commodities. As a result of these changes, the population might seem to have fragmented into a bewildering diversity of markets for consumer goods. As Jameson argues, individual and national identities have been shattered by a global image market which 'reflects . . . the absence of any great collective project.' However, these are ultimately ruled by one 'global totality' (late capitalism) which has relentlessly spread its tentacles across all nations and into all aspects of life. Most theorists of postmodernism are horrified by the idea of sameness, and Jameson likewise fears that late capitalism has squeezed the world into a single system which neutralises individual and cultural differences. In such a world, local cultures cease to have any meaning, impact, or sense of identity, and we all lose our sense of historical and geographical place.

Jameson talks about how we are caught in a mass of 'depthless' and centreless multinational communication networks so vast and complex that it is impossible to mentally grasp them. In doing so, he represents postmodernism in terms of transformations it has made to our relationships to space.

Jameson checks into postmodern space

The way postmodernism alters our experience of space is explored by Jameson in a passage of his book which describes his visit to the Bonaventure Hotel in Los Angeles, designed by John Portman. Although he pays a lot of attention to this one building, Jameson does not see it as one of a kind. He notes that similar points could equally have been made about the Pompidou Centre in Paris or the Eaton Centre in Toronto. You may be able to find in the following summary echoes of buildings you have visited yourself.

A popular building, visited by both locals and tourists, entering it, according to Jameson, is a disorientating experience in itself. It is hard to find the entrances (the one Jameson used seems to go round the back and up a walkway), and you can readily find yourself in a part of the building you did not intend to be in. Once inside, you might struggle to find your way to the reception desk as various passages (and apparently a shortage of signs) send you drifting in the wrong direction. But rather than being a totally frustrating experience, the Bonaventure can be exhilarating. In it you find yourself in a space full of many different pleasures and levels of experience. Escalators and elevators (Jameson describes these as like air-borne gondolas) rise up and down but take you nowhere in particular. Balconies, shops, gardens, columns and gigantic hanging streamers make the interior of the hotel feel like a miniature, self-enclosed city. This is confirmed by the difficulty of finding your way in and by the fact that the building has a reflective glass skin. The effect of these glass walls for Jameson is that, like mirror shades which stop you from seeing people's eyes, they repel the surrounding city, confirming Jameson's view of the place as a little world complete in itself. Trying to make sense of this place, your senses are both stimulated and bewildered as you immerse yourself in a crowded yet superficial 'hyperspace'.

Jameson sees the Bonaventure as symbolic of postmodern times because of the way it mixes in a 'depthless' space many different, fleeting, 'overstimulating' images and experiences. Jameson finds that in this strange space you are literally swept along by corridors and lifts. The building seems able to take over, making you feel passive and complacent as you drift around trying to take it all in. You lose your sense of perspective and place. In the process of being sucked into the building's confusions and charms you lose, according to

Jameson, all capacity for rationally distanced judgement. Everything becomes equal and weightless. In these ways the Bonaventure is taken to be symptomatic of the whole global postmodern experience.

Criticism of Jameson

Jameson defends grand, sweeping social theory against the postmodern faith in modest micropolitics and difference. But critics see the model he provides of the postmodern situation as far too all-embracing.

On the one hand Jameson suggests that postmodern conditions are too huge, complex and merged into everyday life for us to be able to fully comprehend them. On the other hand he reduces this complexity to a single all-powerful system which he thinks can explain everything. His own perspective is so monolithic that he ends up repeating the very flattening of cultural differences that he is out to condemn.

Out of this perspective, Jameson presents isolated objects (a hotel, an Andy Warhol painting) and assumes that you can simply read vast social systems off them. How is this possible? What about the different meanings which those objects might have for people who have no interest in theories of postmodernism and late capitalism?

Linked to these criticisms is the idea that Jameson grants himself too much authority. He argues that under postmodern conditions 'we' have lost our sense of history, but the implication is that his own historical awareness has remained miraculously intact. The rest of us have been mesmerised by the dazzling world of consumer capitalism but Jameson can stand above it all and see this world for what it really is. Where does he get this power from?

This arrogance comes from the belief that a single set of tools (in his case certain Marxist concepts) can be used to (a) explain everything and (b) draw up a template for collective human destiny.

———— Theorising the city ————

The 'post-metropolis' described by Soja, Jameson and others does not come from nowhere. It is built on aspects of urban life which have been present since the early days of the modern city. To this degree the postmodern social situation amplifies rather than radically departs from conditions which have been in place for over one and a half centuries. Because of this, a lot of recent writing about the postmodern city intensifies themes originally developed by early theorists of modernity.

The beginnings of modern forms of society are usually found in the explosion of large-scale urban experience that took place in the middle of the nineteenth century, when over half of the population of England began to live in cities. This soon became the normal course of events as the process of modernisation spread across the world. At the same time a number of writers found that the new city experience highlighted some of the ideas and questions about the self that philosophers had long been exploring. The modern city seemed to live out in concrete terms problems about the relationship between the individual and the collective, for example. With the growth of the city there was a new emphasis on the fragmentary and fluid nature of experience. And with the modern urban lifestyle, individuals (as we saw in Chapter 6) became more self-conscious about their way of life, more concerned about their social role, and more anxious about their place in the world.

Lyotard continues this theme. He draws inspiration for his ideas from the kinds of cosmopolitan experience offered by Jameson's world of global media, travel and corporations. In an often quoted passage, he writes with a mixture of excitement and disapproval that:

> � clecticism is the degree zero of culture: one listens to reggae, watches a Western, eats McDonald's (sic) food for lunch and local cuisine for dinner, wears Paris perfume in Tokyo and retro clothes in Hong Kong; knowledge is a matter for TV games. ❊
>
> *The Postmodern Condition*, page 76

It is worth remembering that Lyotard has grave doubts about this kind of mix-and-match approach to culture. As the reference to game shows indicates, he regrets that too often it can lead to complacency. Everything can become too easy, too flat, too wishy-washy. There is no room for struggle. (It is also interesting to note that part of this regret comes from his feeling that in this 'period of slackening' art no longer has a special status.)

One writer more enthusiastic about the kind of picture Lyotard paints is the British critic Iain Chambers. Unlike Fredric Jameson's image of the postmodern 'cultural dominant' as rather all-powerful and unchanging, Chambers' description of life in postmodern space emphasises qualities like vibrancy, flux, experimentation and discontinuity. Chambers does not attempt to provide a complete map of this space and thinks that it would be impossible to do so (see the section on critical modesty below). But he explores in often exciting prose the many ways in which different pockets and levels of reality can overlap, intersect, (sometimes violently) conflict and rub shoulders with each other. In the following passage he continues the theme of cultural mixing that was touched on by Lyotard, but adds to it a concern with how different ethnic, racial and cultural groups can co-exist:

❝ . . . many young black Britons of both sexes sport fashionable Italian track suits and, remixing the examples of New York B-Boys (and Girls) with Jamaican roots, reggae rhythms with rap anthems, dub with scratch, electronic grammar with British syntax, have transformed the multi-ethnic traditions of a once colonial and colonized subject into local and more immediate sense. It suggests a black integration, not so much with the white mainstream as with the wider possibilities of present day metropolitan culture. Diverse *roots* are now displaced and transformed into particular *routes* through the present. ❞

Iain Chambers *Border Dialogues; Journeys in Postmodernity*
(1990) page 75

—— Local versus global culture ——

In our discussions of Soja and Jameson we noted that the new spaces of postmodernity feature a complicated interaction between universal and regional factors. On the one hand there is the continuing expansion of global markets for music, fashion and so on, coupled with the growth of boundary-crossing media and communications systems. On the other hand there is a heightened sensitivity to regional and particular issues of the kind championed by Lyotard and de Certeau. The apparent contradiction between these two aspects – which we can can perhaps translate as a dynamic tension between sameness and difference – can be seen as one of the defining features of the postmodern landscape and is explored below.

Shifting boundaries

Rather like Fredric Jameson, David Morley and Kevin Robins (in their book *Spaces of Identity*) suggest that global satellite and cable broadcasting systems have created a postmodern environment which has changed the shape of national, ethnic and cultural identities. Echoing Gilles Deleuze and Felix Guattari's idea of 'deterritorialisation' (see Chapter 7), they argue that recent technologies of communication and transport have created new geographies based less on the physical boundaries of the land and more on the flow of information and images. In postmodernity, people, information, images and objects migrate around the globe. In the process they make it harder to define the limits of a community or a nation. National and even natural boundaries are still there, of course, but they do not even begin to tell the whole story. They are constantly over-ridden and undermined by 'spaces of transmission' with boundaries of their own. Thus the old categories of national, racial and cultural identity must be balanced by the greater 'symbolic boundaries of language and culture' provided by the mass media, global markets, computerisation and the rest.

Morley and Robins argue that although these new geographies have brought about a crisis in the idea of the nation they have at the same time created a new awareness of regional locations and activities. For example, there has been a growth of local and specialist radio stations as the airwaves have become progressively more deregulated. On one level the entertainment industries are controlled by a shrinking number of multinational companies (film production and distribution is a good example of this monopolisation). On another level, the media are expected to maximise consumer choice. Again, the spread of the Internet over an ever wider area and into ever more homes and institutions has similarly created a mind-boggling range of special-interest web sites. Finally, a television channel broadcasts the same programme to millions of sets at once, but that programme will be seen in many different kinds of places by many different kinds of people and in many different kinds of ways. In all of these cases what we see is a complex combination of global 'electronic communities' and small- scale concerns.

Globalised identities

The American critic George Lipsitz has touched on similar themes. He has agreed that social changes of the kind outlined by Soja, Jameson, Morley and Robins have changed identities and culture. But he argues that these changes have to be measured against the many continuing forms of oppression and inequality to which many people are still subjected. The late capitalist world of mass consumption, computers and multinational communications can hardly be said to affect everybody equally.

Lipsitz has looked at how hip-hop and rap music have taken root in many different countries across the world. Originally rising from the ghettoes of North America, hip-hop and rap records are now listened to the world over. As Lipsitz says, it as though the whole world is listening to what happens in the South Bronx. Lipsitz contends that African cultures have historically been dispersed by the movement of low-wage black labourers from country to country; it is through the production, distribution and consumption of popular music that ethnic and cultural identity can be restored and expressed. Thus a form of music with its source in a very specific region has become the basis of an imaginary global community that crosses national boundaries. Moreover, it is a form of music that plunders from and mixes together a whole range of influences. For instance, many rhythms and samples can be taken from the history of black music (e.g. jazz, soul, funk) and combined with bits and pieces borrowed from mainstream white culture (e.g. news broadcasts, film soundtracks).

A criticism of Lipsitz

Paul Gilroy has criticised Lipsitz's optimistic view for implying that particular kinds of music intrinsically belong to particular ethnic groups. In the first place, you need to take into account the fact that hip-hop can be listened to by white middle-class schoolchildren in rural areas as well as by disadvantaged black youths in the inner cities. In other words you cannot expect any form of music to stay within the boundaries of a single identifiable audience. In the second place one of the points of sampling, scratching and re-mixing is to undermine the idea that culture is the property of a single group.

Finally, Gilroy argues that seeing hip-hop and rap as authentic forms of racial expression denies the fluid and contradictory character of identity by implying that a certain kind of outlook or experience is fundamentally and essentially 'black'. The postmodern world is multi-cultural, interfacial and eclectic: in such a world identities and lifestyles can, like contemporary black music itself, be collages of many different influences. They can be far too fragmentary and fleeting to permit any appeal to an underlying ethnic nature.

Post-coloniality

One of the most important facts about the postmodern geography outlined by Lyotard, Soja and others is that the world is becoming 'post-colonial'. What this means is that the political map of imperialism and colonisation across the world is in the process of being redrawn. While it would be a serious exaggeration to suggest that the world has now got over colonialism (Native Americans, to take just one example, would dispute the idea: post-colonialism cannot mean the same thing for everybody), it is safe to say that the world has recently witnessed the meltdown of empires. The progressive shrinking and weakening of the British Empire is a good example of this. In other cases the idea of the post-colonial situation has more to do with the fact that across the world people seem to be becoming more migrant. Thus the notion that the world is witnessing post-colonial times suggests that important changes are taking place on an international scale in political, economic and social areas. The postmodern spaces described by Soja, Jameson and Gilroy are part of these changes: they are physical or imaginary spaces in which different voices converge, and can be seen as post-colonial in the sense that they seem to erode the rigorous boundaries of nationality and race.

The idea of the post-colonial also refers to the theory and in some cases the practice of marginal voices getting a say in representation. This version of post-colonialism is about how the arts and media can and should respond to life in an interracial, multi-ethnic world. Thinkers often classed as post-colonial in this way include Edward Said, Homi Bhabha and Gayatri Spivak. We cannot do justice to their work in the space available, but we can note their main concerns in a general way.

Who speaks?

You may have noticed that in this book I have had a tendency to use plurals in what may seem like unusual places. I have written at various points of knowledges, histories, and sexualities. This may seem to be merely an annoying grammatical quirk on my part (and it is a usage not recognised by the spell-check on my word processor), but it follows the current practice of many theorists influenced by the terms of postmodernism. We have seen throughout this book a general sensitivity within postmodernism to the issue of difference, and the perceived need to speak in the plural of things which once seemed perfectly happy to be singular is part of this concern (seen particularly in the work of Lyotard) to preserve diversity at all costs. To speak of sexualities, for example, is to recognise that not all sexuality expresses the same thing or arises from the same impulse. Feminist critics, among others, have argued that the universal desire or urge implied by generalised talk of sexuality is actually a male heterosexual idea. Or again, to speak of history is to deny that what passes as an objective or 'true' account of historical events might be open to different interpretations by different groups with different interests. It implies that you have access to the only correct version. By referring to multiple histories, you suggest that no single overview can do justice to the full complexity of historical events and their effects, and you raise the question of whose history is being told. Speaking in the plural in this way acknowledges that diverse outlooks and experiences always exist to disrupt total or global theory.

This is just one of the effects that the growing awareness of diversity has had within the humanities. It can be seen as part of a general sense of caution which postmodernism has brought to the study of culture and society. One major concern which comes out of this is the need to ask of any act of representation (whether a film, a news story, a photograph or a novel): Who is being allowed to speak in this representation, for whom, and to what end? Who 'hears' it and who is excluded from it?

Critics informed by the 'posts' argue that it is preferable not to speak on behalf of oppressed, under-privileged or marginalised people. All groups should have access to means by which they can represent their own concerns and experiences. Speaking for others is a form of 'grammatical violence', as Lyotard would say. By doing it you will inevitably (and however unconsciously) invest them with your own prejudiced values and outlooks. This brings us to the next point.

Sensitivity to centrisms

Back in the early 1980s a group of musicians in the UK released a hit charity record in aid of famine relief called 'Do They Know it's Christmas?' Its lyric tugged on the nation's heartstrings by pointing out that starving children in Ethiopia would not be sampling the joys of the festive season that year. However, Great Britain could become Santa Claus by buying the records and delivering to Africa the 'greatest gift they'll get this year [which] is life'. The problem with this idea is that there was no reason why the starving in Ethiopia *should* have known that it was Christmas time at all. Christmas as we know it is hardly a universal idea; many of its traditions are European and quite recent in origin, a large proportion of the world's religions do not recognise it and even in countries that do celebrate it there is a great diversity of customs. Thus the question raised by the title of the song was entirely European in origin. In other words it was Eurocentric. Similar cases of Eurocentrism can be found in many ideas about 'primitive' as opposed to 'civilised' cultures, and in exotic portrayals of 'the orient' as a mysterious land full of eastern promise. The way the globe is often divided into first, second and third 'worlds' works in much the same way: in what sense do Ethiopians living in Ethiopia, for example, feel themselves to be living in the 'third world'?

You may remember from our discussion of Jacques Derrida in Chapter 5 that postmodern theory is always on its guard against centres. This concern is sometimes reflected by the desire to uncover various centrisms of the kind noted above. So post-colonial critics look for evidence of Eurocentrism in the media and literature. Others look for the hidden signs of 'phallocentrism' (having a 'masculine' bias), 'heterocentrism' (having a heterosexual bias) and any number of other 'centrisms' in seemingly innocent texts.

Critical modesty

As a result of the above influences, and many other of the postmodern issues outlined in this book, critics are now often much more cautious about the kinds of value judgement they make. The British sociologist Zygmunt Bauman has called this a change in the perceived role of intellectuals from being 'legislators' to 'interpreters'. What he means is that academics are becoming reluctant to put forward moral or aesthetic distinctions between what is 'good' and what is 'bad'. My own use of inverted commas around these words echoes this sense of caution.

Intellectuals begin to renounce their own authority. Instead of trying to lead us to how things *should be* (as though, superior to the rest of us, they know what is good for us) they are now more inclined to spend their time modestly probing the way things *seem* to be. In postmodernism, we become so aware of the existence of other different points of view – and of the historically and socially limited nature of our own – that treading carefully increasingly appears to be crucial.

Through the work of Lyotard, Derrida and many others we learn to forget the idea of universal values. As old certainties start to crumble, there is a tendency to feel that all views are equally valid. With the fall of the grand metanarratives (Lyotard) more attention is paid to the 'little narratives' of regional issues and everyday life. The commonplace is converted into culture. There arrives a cloud of relativism and a flurry of deliberately 'weak thought'. This last phrase belongs to the Italian philosopher Gianni Vattimo. Partly recalling the writings of Jean Baudrillard, he argues that the age of mass communications produces such an 'apparently irresistible pluralization' that we have been released from the shackles of once authoritative principles of reality. As Baudrillard himself has argued, the media are so saturated with information, and with so many different voices demanding to be heard, that it is no longer possible to know what you either know or want any more. In postmodernism, value systems and identities become so multiple and so tenuous that a humble, more open approach to philosophy is necessary which lets go of whatever hold it once thought it had on the truth.

From the centre to the margin

Postmodern and/or post-colonial theory seeks to free up the means of representation for the voices of those others normally pushed to the edges of mainstream cultural expression. In doing so it aims to shatter all 'centric' accounts of history, culture and society and to open up an infinitely more plural, inclusive mixture of world views.

Part of this project involves studying texts which capture something of the deterritorialised nature of postmodern geography. Salman Rushdie's *The Satanic Verses* (first published in 1988) has been read in this light by Gayatri Spivak. She sees it as a telling portrait of the postmodern feeling of fractured and plural cultural identity. In its uneasy mixture of eastern and western traditions Rushdie's novel contains an unresolvable tension between the author's experience of a migrant, hybrid way of life and his sense of belonging to a specific nationality. The feeling of openness, liberty and boundary-blurring which can, as we have seen, be offered by the new postmodern spaces of supersonic travel, migration and media is accompanied by a contradictory sensitivity to the edges between different cultures. Again, there is the sense that in the postmodern map of the world we live on the sometimes jarring, sometimes merging borders between the global and the local, the fluid and the fixed, the old and the new.

Spivak also notes that it is now impossible not to read *The Satanic Verses* in the light of the fatwa issued by the Ayatollah Khomeini in 1989. The novel has become entwined in the sometimes violent disputes and protests that have surrounded it. Many Muslims felt that Rushdie's supposedly postmodern mixing of fact and fiction and east and west, was part of a blasphemous conspiracy against Islam: it brought cultural plurality and mixing into what they saw as the decidedly *un*mixed historical truth and integrity of the prophet Muhammad's revelation. Rushdie's aim had been to express the doubt that characterises life in our times as we become ever more aware of different people's histories, views and needs. The problem was that for some Muslims such a state of uncertainty did not apply to their system of beliefs. With the issue of the fatwa and the subsequent conflicts surrounding it, *The Satanic Verses* was both an expression and a victim of post-colonial insecurity.

The fact that such insecurity was thought by some not to apply to their faith asks some awkward questions:

- Does anybody have the right to criticise other people's beliefs?

- Do postmodernists have the right to urge other people to embrace *their* beliefs?

- Can postmodernism tell us anything useful about the experiences of people whose world view is *not* as hybrid and cosmopolitan as that of postmodern theorists?

- If postmodernism is a 'global' social condition, does it affect all people in the same way?

In short, it expresses what is perhaps the fundamental (and impossible to resolve) concern of postmodernism – the difficulty of living with difference.

— And finally . . . an inconclusion —

It has been suggested by some that the great virtue of the term 'postmodernism' is that it is so imprecise. Although it has now been around for a long time, it still refuses to settle down or solidify into a single meaning. As we have seen, one of postmodernism's recurring themes is this very instability of meaning: meanings, it is argued, are never unified; they are at all levels disrupted by difference. To this extent we might say that postmodernism practices what it preaches in that it continues to mean different things to different people, and to have a sometimes bewildering range of applications in different areas. It remains stubbornly elusive. In this way it allows ideas to stay mobile, constantly re-inventing themselves and adjusting to changing circumstances.

So it is difficult to write a satisfactory conclusion for this book. Because so many of the topics we have addressed remain open-ended, there is no simple way of tying all the loose ends together or of closing the case. Theorists like Derrida, Lyotard and the rest would at any rate suggest that this is how it should be, and would resist the idea that their work can be summarised in one easy package. Nevertheless, that is what I have tried to do.

My conclusion is therefore, in keeping with the subjects explored in this chapter, a modest one. I hope I have given you a taste of how the term postmodernism, however slippery and contradictory it might be, offers a way into debates about contemporary societies, cultures and lifestyles. I also hope that you now feel able to tackle them head-on by reading some of the theorists we have discussed directly.

'Postmodernism' may not be the most appropriate name for our times. Sometimes other words could perhaps have done a far better job, and in the future much more useful terms are likely to be found. Yet many of the issues it currently names are likely to remain constant. In some cases they will probably intensify. I therefore believe that certain claims recently made about us reaching the 'end' of postmodernism are not only premature, but distract attention away from some of the important challenges it can raise.

INDEX